NOTHING BUT BLUE SKIES

TIM KEOGH

keoboy

Published by Keoboy Publications.

Email. keoboy@fsmail.net

Printed and bound by Deanprint, Stockport, Cheshire.

Cover by Michael Bradbury.

Cover photo and other Man City photos © The Manchester Evening News. Author photos © Tim Keogh.

ISBN: 978-0-9562881-0-3

For Lisa

Contents.

ONE

DOWN EVERY STREET IN MANCHESTER.

It was the summer of 1966. World Cup Willie, Bobby Moore, Bobby Charlton, Sir Alf Ramsey, Geoff Hurst, a Russian linesman, and Ken Wolstenholme uttering those immortal lines " There are some people on the pitch, they think it's all over….. it is now." On the contrary it was only just beginning.

The first day of a brand new season. My first football match. The sun was shining and the grass had never been greener. I clutched dad's hand tightly as we joined the multitudes making their way, like figures in a Lowry painting, through the docklands and warehouses towards Old Trafford, the home of Manchester United. I watched in complete awe as the bridge over the Ship Canal rose into the heavens to allow the passage of one of Manchester's Liners on its way to some distant land. Manchester United versus West Bromwich Albion. The holy trinity of Best, Law and Charlton. The sea of Red, the roar of the Stretford End and a thrilling United victory by five goals to three. Life doesn't get much better than this, dad must have said as we breathlessly made our way home. I didn't reply, not wishing to sound ungrateful, but amidst the explosion of colour and noise, I, perhaps alone among a crowd of 41000, remained curiously unmoved on that distant August afternoon.

Saturday 8th October 1966. This is where it all began for me. Fresh from a week of trying to win a Blue Peter badge or indeed a Crackerjack pencil, Dad, brother Pete and I found ourselves on Fountain Street just around the corner from the Tudor House café in Middleton Gardens. I looked across at the Palace cinema trying to make out what film they were showing. Dad, being a great fan of westerns, had already taken us to see "Geronimo" and "The Return of the Magnificent Seven" earlier in the summer. I could hardly contain myself as we waited for the Yelloways coach to take us via Every Street in Manchester to Maine Road, the home of Manchester City Football Club, for the afternoon's match with Tottenham Hotspur. The radio on the coach told us that the Beatles were living in a yellow submarine and the boys on the back row were warning one and all not to go to West Brom as they had foot and mouth. Funny, as only a few weeks earlier they had seemed fine! The man sitting directly behind us asked his friend who City were playing that afternoon. To an eight year old like myself this seemed totally incomprehensible. After all I had spent the last three sleepless nights worrying about the tactics of today's opponents and how City were going to overcome them!

The coach made its slow progress through the myriad of terrace streets that constituted Moss Side past the back entry where Grandad Keogh had parked his bicycle for 6d since 1923. Dad was a Red, which explained our earlier excursion to Old Trafford, but his father James had supported the Blue side of Manchester since coming over from Ireland to work as a barman in the Temple public house in Cheetham Hill. It was another temple that loomed up out of the Manchester mist and drizzle on that October day. The Kippax Street Stand was a huge covered terrace that unusually ran lengthways alongside the pitch at Maine Road, and housed some 26000 rabid Manchester City fans. Avoiding the huge pools of water

8

and the piles of dung from the immense police horses ostensibly guarding the handful of Tottenham Hotspur coaches Pete and I entered the Junior turnstile scarily parted from dad for a few anxious minutes. We bought a programme for sixpence and then, considerably relieved at being rejoined by dad, walked right along the back of the Kippax Stand before entering the extra solitary turnstile leading to the Platt Lane seats. I could hardly contain my excitement as I climbed up what seemed like hundreds of steps. Emerging at the top there it was in front of me. A green carpet as far as the eye could see, illuminated at each corner by four huge floodlights. It literally took my breath away.

In the half hour that remained until kick off we eagerly devoured the programme which told us among other things that a really good meal could be obtained at the UCP restaurant on Market Street, that DJ Jimmy Saville would fix it at the Top Ten Club every Sunday at Belle Vue Zoo Park, and that it cost 37 shillings and 6 pence to take the train to watch City at Newcastle the following Saturday, departing from Manchester Exchange station.

The Sky Blue of the shirts illuminated by the lights on this dank, drizzly afternoon, combined with the swell of the grumbling human tide to our right on the Kippax Street terrace proved to be a heady mix for an impressionable eight year old. The chimney pots on the roofs of houses above the tunnel by the corner flag seemed almost within reach, and the invalid carriages stationed in all four corners were appropriately coloured sky blue. I wondered whether Away supporters would have carriages in their own team's colours. A few yards in front of us stood Harry Dowd the City goalkeeper dressed in a green jumper, black shorts and black socks.

Dad told us that he scored a goal for City from open play a couple of years earlier in the days before substitutes were allowed. I hung on dad's every word and Dowd immediately took on a god-like status. The only disadvantage from sitting behind the goal was that the other end seemed miles away, and a City goal could only be confirmed by the fact that every body stood up as one cheering their heads off.

City had just been promoted from the old Second Division and after ten games were sixth from the bottom with eight points whereas Tottenham were riding high in second place with fifteen (only two points for a win in those days!). The City side contained the likes of skipper Tony Book, Elvis Presley look-a-like Glyn Pardoe, mister dependable Alan Oakes, the great "Nelly" Young and soon to be icons Mike Summerbee and Colin Bell. All of whom were to become part of the Championship side the following year, which to this day remains City's greatest team. They were joined that afternoon by the lesser lights of Jimmy Murray, Harry Dowd, George Heslop, Stan Horne and the soon to be released talisman Johnny Crossan, who had been a key figure in the promotion season. Fringe members of the squad included Matt Gray, Alan Ogley and Ralph Brand. The Tottenham side was littered with household names such as Pat Jennings, Mike England, Dave Mackay, Terry Venables and the brilliant Jimmy Greaves. Yet it was the biblically named Frank Saul that made the most impression on me, perhaps due to my imminent conversion to following Manchester City, or more likely to the fact that his distinctive mop of blonde hair stood out in the floodlights amidst the gloom. The crowd was muted, the weather awful, the game unremarkable with City losing 2-1 but as for me, well I was hooked. Was it the sky blue of the shirts? Or perhaps the atmosphere around the stadium? It did not seem as highly charged as my previous visit to Old Trafford. Whatever it was, I was utterly transformed! A Manchester City fan for life!

On the coach journey home Mr. Johnson, who worked at the Gasworks in Middleton, reminded me to tell my mum that we had been down Every Street in Manchester and this was why we were late! We trudged in to find mum ironing and the tea ready, or this is how it always seemed in the Keogh household. Just another Hard Day's Night for mum I am afraid.

I soon learned a few lessons in amateur psychology from mum who told me that the best time to ask dad if Pete and I could go to another City match was on Friday night after his weekly drink with his pals. Obviously I could not have stayed up so late to actually ask him, (I had been allowed to stay up in the summer to a quarter past nine to watch the end of the evening World Cup matches), so instead I left written messages for him on the mantelpiece on his return from the Old Boars Head, The Railway or some other local hostelry. This tactic worked on two further occasions that season against Newcastle and Everton in which City gained three points, with goals from two of my new heroes Colin Bell and Neil Young.

1967 gave birth to a Summer of Love, A Whiter Shade of Pale, and Sergeant Pepper's Lonely Hearts Club Band, but all of these would assume greater importance much later for the Keogh brothers who only had one thing on their minds – the beautiful game. Replica kits adorned with the name of the club sponsor on the front and the player on the back were unheard of. We badgered mum and dad to buy us sky blue football shirts, white shorts and pale blue socks with maroon tops. The shorts and socks were relatively easy to find but mum looked in vain for City shirts.

Eventually she settled on some sky blue polo shirts from Oldham market as the nearest to the real thing that we were going to get. We asked mum to sew numbers on our backs (mine was number seven after Summerbee and Pete's was number three after Pardoe). We were "thrilled to bits" as we took our new Casey ball with yellow laces onto the field next to the Coop store, which doubled up as Wembley and Maine Road. As the ball became wet it weighed half a ton and the yellow laces made deep lacerations on your forehead if you had the temerity to actually head it! Our street games of British Bulldog, Rally-vo, and Knock-a-door Run were now replaced by important Sixth Round Cup ties played out between City and West Ham, Chelsea, Sheffield United, or whoever we decided would be the opponents on that particular day. Heroes such as Batman, Robin, The Penguin, and even James Bond had to take a back seat. We silenced our Johnny Seven guns, confined our toy soldiers to barracks and our Hornby train sets to the sidings. Collecting Airfix models and Monkees cards were superseded by securing Typhoo Tea colour pictures of our new heroes such as Bobby Tambling, Alan Birchenall and Derek Dougan. At Christmas the Topical Times Soccer Annual took pride of place. We were football crazy, football mad.

Meanwhile at Maine Road the management team of Joe Mercer, who had to leave his previous post at Villa due to illness, and his flamboyant young assistant coach Malcolm Allison, whose playing career ended early owing to injury, both had something to prove, if only to themselves. They placed their trust in their wily skipper Tony Book at right full back, who himself reached the First Division in his mid-thirties via Bath City and Plymouth Argyle. Glyn Pardoe and Mike Doyle were dropped back into the defence and a left winger with a reputation as a troublemaker by the name of Tony Coleman was signed from Doncaster Rovers. The pieces of the jigsaw were beginning to be put in place and by the end of September 1967 City were fifth in the league only two points off the top. It was then that Dad announced one evening after tea that as my ninth birthday treat we would be going to the Manchester derby on Saturday afternoon. Manchester City versus Manchester United. A full house of 63500! The Blues against the Reds!

Dad had been promoted at work resulting in the purchase of our first family car, an Austin 1100 registration number 7619DK. As he drove home from the garage mum proudly stood in the window with her three impressionable sons (Paul the newest addition was born in 1964) awaiting the homecoming hero. As he rounded the corner all three of us let out a cheer worthy of a ninetieth minute cup final winning goal, but the roar soon stuck in our throats when, as if a ghostly linesman's flag had been raised, he proceeded to knock down the gatepost.

The car duly repaired, we said goodbye to Yelloways coaches and set off very early for Maine Road and parked in one of the tiny cobbled streets near the ground. "Mind your car, sir?" asked the winner of a hundred yard dash between three tall West Indian teenagers. It was customary to pay a shilling or two for the privilege of parking in their street and foolhardy to either refuse or suggest paying after the game. Tales of finding your car propped up on bricks or worse upon your return were commonplace.

We took up our position not in the Platt Lane seats, but in the corner of the Kippax Street Stand next to the tunnel by the open Scoreboard End. Dad positioned us on the wall and told us of bygone days in the fifties when children were passed over everybody's heads down to the front where a better view could be obtained. The September sun was shining directly into my face, which I reasoned could cause a problem or two later on for the goalkeepers. But I kept these thoughts to myself. The programme, which now cost a shilling, was the first to contain colour in the inside pages (but this only consisted of a Sky Blue and Red block of colour behind the team line-ups). Pre-match entertainment was supposed to be provided by Pye recording stars Margo and the Marvettes, but by far the biggest laugh was instead supplied by City's new signing from Stockport County goalkeeper Ken Mulhearn. He had only been signed earlier that week and must have been as nervous as me that afternoon. In the pre-match warm up right in front of us he athletically left his goal line to collect a soft cross from a team mate and the ball sailed right through his outstretched arms and trickled into the advertising boards behind the goal. The United fans standing to our right, many in number, could hardly contain themselves. Perhaps he had lost the ball in the bright sunshine? Nevertheless, I squirmed in acute embarrassment and felt sick at the prospect of Ken keeping a United side containing Denis Law, George Best and Bobby Charlton at bay.

City came out of the traps and threw everything at United. After only a few minutes Colin Bell scored and I looked at Dad as if to say that the times they were a changing, which I couldn't have anyway because I had never heard of Bob Dylan. But as if in a nine year olds' worst nightmare marksman Neil Young hobbled off injured and Bobby Charlton scored two for the Reds to win the game for United. Dad looked at me as if to say, "this is how it is, son". He could have added "And always will be", but dad was not like that. Outside the ground there was a strange feeling of menace in the air that was probably transmitted from dad as he clutched our hands tighter than usual. It seemed to be a case of getting back to the car as quickly as we could and getting back onto Rochdale Road. At that stage I had never heard of hooliganism but I sensed that all was not quite right. I returned home to a subdued birthday tea before reading the print off both the match programme and the local Football Pink newspaper (in the days when it really was pink). "There's always another match" reassured mum as I made the lonely walk up to bed. I silently shook my head. She just did not understand.

In our house Sunday morning meant only one thing – the whole family went along to Mass in the local church. Some years earlier it had been held in the pub behind our house! At that time United was known as the Catholic club in Manchester and all the local priests were keen followers. I went through the motions of mumbling through my prayers that Sunday when the priest paused in his sermon to wonder why " young Keogh is looking so downhearted this morning after yesterday's game?" To be publicly humiliated at such a young age was particularly hard to take, but it was also character building and would hopefully stand me in good stead for what lay ahead in a lifetime of following Manchester City. Yet I did not look at this priest ever again in the same way. He seemed to have identified me as an opponent and deep down this struck home. This particular defeat by United must have been rare because City were really flying that year. I saw them put six past Leicester and five past Sheffield United but the game that everyone still talks about was the so-called "ballet on ice" against Tottenham Hotspur that took place on the 9th of December.

The narrow streets around the ground were treacherous and the pitch was covered in ice and snow as we took our seats in the Platt Lane End. There would be no way that a game would be played today in such conditions. I was amazed to see that an orange ball was being used and asked dad why Jimmy Greaves was lining up on the right wing at kick off as opposed to his normal role as Inside Right. Dad explained that due to the sun peeping through the corner of the Main Stand this was the only strip of turf that was green and soft as opposed to the rest of the pitch that was bone hard. He reasoned that this would probably provide a better footing for Greaves with Spurs attacking the Platt Lane End. This insight had dad in my eyes a football genius as after only five or six minutes he scampered through to score past Mulhearn and put Spurs one up. City included in their ranks their new signing Francis Lee who had cost a then record £60000 from Bolton a few weeks earlier. As Spurs began to slip and slide City appeared to glide over the surface and goals from Mike Summerbee, Tony Coleman, Neil Young and Colin Bell gave City a four-one win. Their appearance on Match Of The Day that night got everybody sitting up and taking notice of this team from the other side of Manchester! The forward line of Lee, Bell, Summerbee, Young and Coleman was beginning to send a shiver throughout the defences of the whole country, and would soon become etched into the folklore of this great club.

A fan always remembers the first team that he watches with particular affection, and although hundreds of players have donned the sky blue shirt since that season, some with more distinction than others, even the bit-part players from this squad linger in the memory. There was a young promising outside right called Paul Hince who played a few games before disappearing via Charlton Athletic and Bury only to re-emerge many years later as the football correspondent for the Manchester Evening News (his pen being much mightier than his right foot). The extremely talented Stan Bowles broke into the side that year and would go on to have a fantastic career with QPR and England. There was an inside forward called John Clay, a promising striker called Chris Jones, and of course Dave Connor who played far more games than the other youngsters put together. Dave Connor was a local lad, a hard man in the mould of Tommy Smith, Norman Hunter or Ron "Chopper" Harris. He was not the sort of player that we emulated on the Coop field in our games of Wembley but he had an important role to play in this all-conquering swashbuckling Man City side. He was brought in to stop the opposition playing, to mark a skilful opponent out of the game, and then to give the ball to the likes of Colin Bell who would do the rest.

Just before Christmas 1967 was a time of great upheaval for the Keogh family. We moved house to Alkrington, a more affluent part of Middleton populated in the main by an army of secondary school teachers, lecturers from the nearby De La Salle College, and successful North Manchester businessmen. I must have been a rather precocious nine year old because with the van loaded up and the family all waiting I had a last misty-eyed walk around all the rooms in the house. It was as if we were going to India or some other colonial outpost instead of only three miles across town. The Air-Raid siren at the local primary school still in use some twenty years after the end of the Second World War sounded a farewell salute as the removal van slowly pulled away from the house. The weather was wet, foggy and miserable and the mood did not lift at the

17

weekend as City lost twice to West Brom, these being their only defeats in twenty games.

The gloom was lifted in January by my next visit to Maine Road to watch my first F.A. Cup tie against Reading, then in the Third Division. I was a little anxious due to the fact that I wouldn't be going with dad but with Sean, a friend from our old street and his grandma who seemed to be just this side of eighty and resembled the famous actress Margaret Rutherford. On the way to the match Sean related how his house had recently been burgled and that the thief forced entry via the kitchen, stole three tomatoes and promptly made his getaway obviously in a bid not to get caught red-handed. City ran out in their unfamiliar away strip of maroon shirts and shorts and we sat back to await the massacre. Our seats were on the front row just to the side of the net at the Platt Lane end. The rain was relentless, the pitch was becoming treacherous and Reading brought City down to their level. All of a sudden Francis Lee was upended right in front of us and City were awarded a penalty. As Francis was getting to his feet and tightening his laces winger Tony Coleman grabbed hold of the ball, placed it on the spot and then promptly blasted it high over the bar. A game which City had been expected to win easily ended goalless, although the replay a few days later finished with the Blues scoring seven without reply.

City were knocked out of the Cup three weeks later by the odd goal in seven in a replay at Leicester and as the saying goes were able to concentrate on the League. With ten games to go there was everything to play for, and after a fantastic victory at Old Trafford by three goals to one at the end of March the finishing line was in sight. With Colin Bell

18

returning to the side after injury the Blues secured a dour nil-nil draw at Molineux against Wolves before three straight wins over Sheffield Wednesday, Everton and Tottenham Hotspur.

The League title came down to the very last day of the season with City travelling to Newcastle and United at home to Sunderland, with both sides level on points. Two goals from Neil Young and one each from Summerbee and Lee gave City a famous victory by four goals to three while United unexpectedly lost at home to Sunderland. The only downer came that night when I was allowed to stay up late to watch "Match Of the Day". I sat for hours in my City scarf and bobble hat waiting for that distinctive title music with the Football Pink on my knee. But what a let down! When the "Match of the Day" title music ended pictures were immediately beamed from Old Trafford for the highlights of the title decider between Manchester United and Sunderland! It was obvious that the BBC had decided who they thought would win the league. Their cameras were at Old Trafford! In those days there was only one main match shown and that night of all nights it wasn't to be City. Nevertheless, in only my second season as a Blue City were the League champions! What a feeling!

Eighth birthday presents. Table football and a Man City bobble hat.

TWO.

TOMMY BOOTH WAS A VERY NICE LAD.

My favourite City song of the time was "Sha-La-La-La-Summerbee"(adapted from the Small Faces hit). In August 1968 this was replaced in my affections when The Beatles released the classic "Hey Jude". In no time at all its fantastic ending was taken up by the Blues fans on the Kippax. But even this could not inspire the team as they began the defence of the title in poor form winning only one of the first nine games. By October I was thrilled to see that Harry Dowd had managed to win back his place in the City goal and a young centre half from Middleton, Tommy Booth, began to make his name at centre half in place of George Heslop. Dad proudly informed us on every possible occasion that he had taught Tommy at school on the Langley estate some years earlier, and that he was a "very nice lad". Tommy immediately rose in my estimation, and I began to talk about him as if he was a member of the family.

On December 7th grandad joined us in the Platt Lane Stand for the game against Burnley. Tony Book was due to be out injured for some time so City purchased, according to grandad, a "boy" for a record £65000 from a team called Hearts in Scotland. I thought this amazing and was so jealous of this youngster. As City made their way down the tunnel onto the pitch I eagerly scanned each of the players hoping to catch a first glimpse of the boy. Sure enough City had a young mascot at the time called Paul Todd but I could not see the young boy who grandad was referring to as the team warmed up. He put me out of my misery by telling me that this "boy" was in fact Arthur Mann (as in "half a man"!). At the time people were touting Burnley as the team of the Seventies due to the talented youngsters in their ranks such as David Thomas, Martin Dobson, Steve Kindon and their Bobby Charlton look-alike Ralph Coates. But that day they could not live with a rampant City who put seven past them with goals from Doyle, Lee, Bell (2), Young (2), and Coleman. The programme informed us that somebody had lost a "thick nylon hand made bag" and someone else had found a "parcel containing various programmes and a hat", both in the Main stand! Life was so much simpler then.

As 1968 gave way to 1969 despite a real upturn in form and the return of skipper Tony Book from injury it was clear that if City were to be successful it would have to be in the F.A. Cup. After disposing of Luton, Newcastle after a replay, Blackburn and Tottenham, City were drawn against Everton in the semi final at Villa Park. Both teams changed colours that day with Everton wearing Amber and Blue and City their fantastic Red and Black striped kit which was modelled on A.C. Milan and probably Malcolm Allison's idea. I was absolutely thrilled to receive this as my first official football kit and when I wore it for the first time at the park at the top of our road I felt like I was Neil Young! I received the ball from brother Pete, outpacing both my opponents and patches of dog muck, as I glided through the inside left channel before my sweet left foot deposited the ball past the diving keeper just inside the coat which served as the goalpost. Goal……..!!!

It was a tough game at Villa Park and one in which Dave Connor was drafted in to play his usual man-marking game on the effervescent Alan Ball. Needless to say Connor did what he was paid to do and the game appeared to be drifting towards a replay when in the last minute up popped dad's favourite Tommy Booth to score and put City through to Wembley. It would be another five years before mum and dad decided that I was old enough to travel to Wembley but in 1969 I did the next best thing by watching the Final on colour television!

Although dad was a teacher at a secondary school in Salford we were not blessed with today's luxuries. I remember waking in the morning to find the insides of my bedroom window covered in the beautiful patterns fashioned by thick ice due to the fact that we had no central heating. We had a car that usually avoided the gateposts, our holidays consisted of a week on the Fylde Coast usually at Lytham St. Anne's, but it would be some years before we acquired a colour television. One of my more "well-to-do" school friends invited me round to watch the Final on his colour set. The Final was on both BBC and ITV and the build up usually began about nine o'clock in the morning and it was absolutely unmissable from first minute until last. It consisted of highlights from earlier rounds, endless interviews, cup final "Quiz Ball" and "It's A Knockout" with Stuart Hall, Eddie Waring and Arthur Ellis. City were playing a Leicester side who were on the verge of relegation from the First Division yet contained several good players including a very young Peter Shilton, David Nish, Alan "Sniffer" Clarke, and Andy Lochead who looked as hard as nails and at least in his early fifties. They don't make them like him anymore. The game was settled by a goal from Neil Young and City added the F.A. Cup to the League Championship of a year earlier. From the moment that the two teams emerged from the tunnel to be presented to Princess Anne before the match, to the presentation of the trophy to Tony Book, to the interviews and laps of honour every minute is etched in my memory. The Red and Black strip seemed to make it even more exotic. It took me hours to fall asleep that April night in 1969.

The Americans put a man on the moon that summer, The Beatles walked across a Zebra Crossing on Abbey Road in London and I kept my place as school goalkeeper as I entered my final year at Primary School. We won three trophies that season including the prestigious Clayton Cup. Probably our best player was Mark Hilton, who went on to play League football for Oldham Athletic, and I can still hear his dad bellowing from the touchline for what seemed to be the whole ninety minutes – "Give it to our Mark"- and we usually did. The dad of another player when arriving late one Saturday morning greeted my mud covered figure with the following, "What score is it Tim?" When I informed him that we were three goals down he replied, "Can't they find anybody better than you to go in the nets?"

My finest hour as the school goalkeeper took place at St. Malachy's in Collyhurst on the outskirts of Manchester. It was only a six a side tournament which took place on a concrete school yard but we were up against boys from the meanest streets in town and we fought our way through the rounds to the final. All the games were refereed by Man United first teamers and local heroes Brian Kidd and Carlo Sartori who wore their bright red club track suits which would have intimidated some of the greatest sides in Europe, let alone a group of ten year old City fans from Middleton. We were one nil up with only seconds remaining when the opposing striker shot low and hard for the bottom corner. I dived along the concrete to my right but as I felt myself falling the ball hit a defender's heel, which totally changed the direction of the shot. Somehow I managed to twist around and palm the ball to safety before landing with a thud on the floor with what seemed like applause ringing in my ears! Even Gordon Banks would have been proud of such a save.

I really enjoyed Primary school. The teachers were very kind except for the headteacher who was a nun who walked around with a strap in her hand and possessed an icy glare that could cut you in half. I kept out of her way. All my thoughts were concentrated on whether we had just enough boys to make a good game of soccer at lunchtime, and whether I could keep my place on the school team. One particular day though I was placed in a rather sticky situation that I could not quite wriggle out of. There were two cousins in our class, John Rudge and Johnny White, who usually got on really well but for one reason or another had fallen out and there was to be a fight arranged on the field after school. Being a good friend of both lads I was given the job of going around and telling as many people as I could of the time and place of the aforementioned bout. Excitement was reaching a crescendo as the afternoon wore on. We were just about to line up to return to class at the end of afternoon play when Rudge approached me full of consternation. "Keogh", he stammered, " I have just remembered that I can't fight tonight after school as my mum is picking me up to go to the dentist." "But I have told absolutely everybody. There will be hundreds there." I protested. "Well then, you will have to take my place," reasoned Rudge and he left my side before I could reply.

This would be my first ever fight in front of practically the whole school against a boy with whom I had no quarrel whatsoever. And I was regarded as a real swot! I would not have bet a lot on my chances of victory. I was mortified but could not really back out without losing face. As we grappled in the mud all I could see were ankles and scuffed shoes, and all I could hear were muffled roars of encouragement. At one point he was on top of me and I could neither move nor indeed breathe. For a split second I feared that I was a "gonner", but from somewhere I summoned up the strength to knock him off me and in the same movement landed a punch right on his nose spilling blood everywhere. The next thing that I knew was that there was an almighty cheer and it was all over. I had won. The next day Rudge thanked me but I took no pleasure in such a hollow victory.

Having won the F.A. Cup in April, City embarked on their second European adventure hoping to survive this time beyond the First Round. They were drawn against Spanish giants Athletico Bilbao and came away from the First Leg in Spain with a three all draw. I pestered dad for over a fortnight to take me to the return leg, as it was due to be played a couple of days after my birthday. To see a European Cup Winners Cup game under floodlights would be beyond my wildest dreams. To my delight he gave in! Pete was not deemed old enough to accompany us to a night match so it was just dad and me. As soon as we emerged from the car and duly paid our young minder I turned to catch a first glimpse at the floodlights casting eerie shadows across the rooftops of Moss Side. It sent shivers down my back.

As the teams lined up the atmosphere generated by a near 50000 crowd was electric. Bilbao seemed so sophisticated in their red and white stripes, and I could not take my eyes off their keeper the great Iribar clad all in black at the Platt Lane End. At school I was proud to wear my mum's old green Ice Skating jumper in goal but I would have given anything to be dressed all in black like Iribar or, as my dad mentioned, the legendary Russian keeper Lev Yashin. The dream-like evening was made complete as Summerbee began to turn his full back inside out and deliver such teasing crosses into the goalmouth. Bell began to make those surging runs of his into the box. He had such great energy! Francis Lee threatened mayhem every time he was on the ball, and he was so difficult to knock off it. And then there was Neil Young gracefully floating through the inside left channel before unleashing a shot which brought Iribar to his knees. At the back Doyle was tigerish in the tackle and young Tommy Booth played with an elegance way beyond his years. Behind them all Joe Corrigan, though undoubtedly nervous, played with a calm assurance. A trademark thunderbolt from Alan Oakes (they either went in the back of the net or in row 50) and goals from Bell and Bowyer carried City through easy winners on the night. I danced my way back to the car through the inevitable puddles and horse manure not caring if dad obliterated the gatepost on our return!

A new decade dawned with City in indifferent form but with their terrific recent record against the Reds I made my first visit to Old Trafford as a City supporter for the Fourth Round Cup tie on January 24th confident of victory. When I learned that United were without Best and Law I felt that there was no way that City could lose. I should have known better. Dad informed me that I could not wear my treasured City scarf for this match and when we arrived at the top of what is now Sir Matt Busby Way there was not a sky blue favour in sight. It was a sea of Red and White that met us. My stomach turned over. I felt as if everybody knew which team I supported. As we entered the turnstiles things did not get any better. When we took up our places in the Scoreboard Paddock above the tunnel by the corner flag I felt as if I was the only Blue in the ground. I looked apprehensively down the pitch to see the infamous Stretford End and was amazed to note that there were seats behind the terracing. I had not noticed this on the television and it was never mentioned. Perhaps it did not quite fit the image. As the ground filled up a huge feeling of unease swept over me. City, too, were strangely subdued right from the kick off. United hit City with a tidal wave of non-stop attacking and it was no surprise when they took the lead from a Willie Morgan penalty at the Scoreboard End. City huffed and puffed up to half time. On the pitch things were going from bad to worse, and off it I felt totally intimidated and numbed by the presence of the foreign hordes around me. Without actually saying so I longed for the comfort of home. Two goals from Brian Kidd sealed City's fate and we left some minutes before the end of the match without a backward glance.

Although City were struggling in the League and knocked out of the F.A. Cup by United their season was not over as they were making great progress in both the League Cup and the European Cup Winners Cup. A two-legged semi final victory over United, thanks to a massive error from Alex Stepney when he parried an indirect goalbound free kick straight to the feet of Summerbee who promptly scored the winner, set the Blues up for a Final against West Brom.

The weather that week was horrendous and on that Saturday morning there was a fair covering of snow in Middleton as I made my way down to the shops to pick up my Shoot magazine which they kept behind the counter for me. As I was idly thumbing through the pages outside the shop I bumped into a friend of mine from school. We walked across the road into the school playground to join some other boys sliding down a sheet of ice that resembled the Cresta Run. As one or two drifted off for lunch we began to throw snowballs at each other and eventually one or two were thrown at passing cars.

Then suddenly one car screeched to a halt! A man jumped out screaming at us. Everyone ran off in different directions but it was me who he was chasing through the school grounds. A strong arm on my shoulder brought me to a halt. I could not get the words " It wasn't me" out of my throat as he prodded his fingers into my chest. "Give me your name and address son. You don't know who I am, do you? I am the Chief Constable of......". I was convinced that day and for weeks after that he was who he said he was, and every time the phone rang at home and every time somebody interrupted a lesson at school I imagined that it was the police. It could only be a matter of time before I was in shackles and on my way to Australia.

The fact that a much depleted City side came from behind to win the League Cup on a "cabbage patch" that day at Wembley almost passed me by. The highlights of the League Cup Final were traditionally shown the next afternoon on ITV with Brian Moore the commentator. He kept reminding viewers that the poor state of the pitch was due to the fact that the Horse of the Year show had been held on it a few days previously. The conditions were awful as City took the field in red and black with their opponents also wearing their change strip of all white. After only a few minutes West Brom took the lead through Jeff Astle but City replied with goals from Mike Doyle and Glyn Pardoe (wearing the unfamiliar number eleven shirt in the absence of Neil Young). In the light of my imminent incarceration I should have enjoyed every second of that weekend like the last meal of a condemned man, but after buying that Shoot magazine everything else remained a blur, your honour.

As a difficult season in the League began to meander to a close City lost three successive home games and injuries began to bite with both Summerbee and Bell falling victim. Youngsters such as Tony Towers, Frank Carrodus, Derek Jeffries and Willie Donachie were blooded as the Blues "fulfilled" their League fixtures. One of these defeats was on the 21st of March against West Ham on a day of torrential rain. This was the game in which Jimmy Greaves made his debut for the Hammers, an embarrassing 5-1 reverse for the Blues, which included an absolute howler from young Joe Corrigan in the City goal. He kicked the ball out from the edge of the area and turned his back on the play as he made his way back towards his goal line. Unfortunately he had kicked the ball straight to Ronnie Boyce who from about 40 yards promptly volleyed the ball back over Joe's head and into an empty goal! Sadly for Joe the Match of the Day cameras captured the goal for posterity.

Amazingly with all the injuries mounting up City managed to get through to the Final of the European Cup Winners Cup, which was to take place in Vienna against the top Polish side Gornik Zabrze. Incredibly as it may seem, the European Cup Winners Cup Final that season was not televised live owing to the F.A. Cup Final replay between Chelsea and Leeds which took place at Old Trafford on the same night. I had to rely on clips shown on "Sportsnight with Coleman" to witness the goals from Francis Lee and Neil Young which brought the Cup home to Manchester. George Heslop replaced the injured Mike Summerbee and Tony Towers a local youngster who only started six League games that year wore the number eleven shirt. The weather was similar to that of a month earlier against West Ham and the stadium was uncovered leaving the sparse crowd of only 10000 absolutely saturated. It is estimated that four or five thousand Blues made the trip and despite their webbed feet victory ensured a goodnight in Vienna. The season ended in triumph with both the League Cup and now the European Cup Winners Cup to add to the League Championship and F.A. Cup won with great style in the preceding two years. What a fantastic time to be a Man City fan! Life was sweet.

Back Row. Alan Oakes, Neil Young, George Heslop, Ken Mulhearn, Colin Bell, Glyn Pardoe, Mike Summerbee. Front Row. Malcolm Allison, Dave Connor, Francis Lee, Tony Book, Tony Coleman, Mike Doyle, Johnny Hart.

THREE.

OH, RODNEY, RODNEY.

The summer of 1970 was unforgettable with England taking up their place as holders at the World Cup in Mexico! The arrest of England Captain Bobby Moore, the naming of City players Colin Bell and Francis Lee in the England side, the constant references to the heat and altitude, the unearthly kick off times, and of course Gordon Banks's save from Pele. And how could I forget the game in which we were two nil up against the Germans in the Quarter Final only to go out by three goals to two thanks to a howler from replacement goalkeeper Peter Bonetti, and a winner from goal machine Gerd Muller.

But most of all I was in eleventh heaven due to the football of the fantastic Brazilians. There was Felix (who was no cat) in the goals, the grace of Carlos Alberto at full back, the guile of Gerson and Tostao in midfield, the lethal left foot of Rivelino, the pace of Jairzinho on the wing, and of course Pele who remains the greatest footballer that I have ever seen. He narrowly missed as he shot from the half way line, and the way he dummied the keeper! Even the Brazilian fans were like no others. Those fantastic samba rhythms and the beautiful yellow shirted girls that the cameraman lingered on for just that second too long. I think that everybody became a secret Brazil fan and their victory in the final over Italy was quite magnificent! We acted out all the goals day after day on the field across from the shops, which we accessed via a narrow entry (known as a ginnel in North Manchester). When our studs clattered on the paving stones for just a few seconds we could imagine ourselves emerging into the sunlight from a tunnel in Mexico City, only to have our illusions shattered by having to step carefully to avoid the broken glass and beer cans left by the previous evening's under age drinkers.

As summer drew to a close and the World Cup drifted from my memory I began to start to have difficulty getting to sleep. Normally I would fall asleep as soon as my head hit the pillow but this was different. I was about to start at Secondary School!

As the bus stopped outside the Grammar School I could hardly breathe. So many things to remember. I was pushed across the road and swept along a corridor towards the hall. "Don't let anybody see that cap", warned a helpful older boy as I tried to place a foot on the floor in my efforts to remain upstanding, as I looked around in vain for a familiar face. We were placed in Forms and I found myself sat next to the only other boy to come from my Primary School. Strange rituals, new routines and new masters were the order of the day. Oh and they fed us too before putting us back on the buses with three hours of homework and instructions to back all our books for the next day. So that was it then, Grammar School.

At first I felt quite intimidated by the confidence of my classmates as they answered question after question. They seemed to have been here before, or must have had much better teachers than me in Primary School. How would I cope? Did I have the correct books for that day? Was I wearing the right kit? Did I have enough dinner money? Would the Sixth formers stick my head down the toilet and pull out my fingernails before Latin?

The school was a boys Catholic Grammar and run by a band of Christian Brothers, the like of which I had never come across not even in my wildest imaginings. They ranged from the barbaric via the mildly eccentric to the stark raving bonkers. There was the History teacher who asked us in the first moments of the first lesson on the first day " What is History?" When nobody replied he promptly thumped the nearest boy hard on the top of his head and announcing his intentions for the year declared "That boys is History". The stick thin Maths teacher would float along the corridors behind a mountain of books like some kind of human fork lift truck only to hold out his hand as you passed and demand your payment of your weekly football pools money. There was the cockney Biology master who everybody thought was Australian and was dubbed "Skippy" after the bush kangaroo! He had a sticker on the back window of his Morris Minor with the slogan "Ban Cars". Perhaps it was meant to say "Ban Cats", because on one memorable occasion he knocked one down on his way to school, threw it onto the back seat of his car, and while it was still warm he dissected it in front of thirty squeamish twelve year olds.

Most of the staff used either the leather strap or the slipper (which was a training shoe) to administer corporal punishment for the slightest misdemeanour. At least half of every lesson was taken up by these public beatings. The RE teacher, who strangely was not a Brother himself, slippered the whole class in alphabetical order when one young boy impertinently enquired as to how Liverpool had gone on at the weekend. The teacher, a rabid scouser, knew that the boy knew that they had lost!

One of my greatest disappointments was that there was no football played in the school until the Third Year. P.E. and Games consisted of either Rugby or Cross Country running. Being stick thin myself and very tall I had no chance of being selected for one of the three First Year Rugby teams and it soon became very obvious that particularly amongst the P.E. staff the rugby crowd was the in-crowd. For the first time in my life where sport was concerned I felt like an outsider and games became a chore where one was either half killed in the scrum on fields which resembled the Somme, or one was chased for miles along country lanes by savage P.E. staff wielding branches of trees which they were not averse to using against weedy pink chapped legs. Happy days.

The new season dawned with only the addition of Freddie Hill to the City squad. The papers described him as "wily", dad preferred the term "veteran", but to me he was simply dull or even slow. Dad reminded me that he had represented England in his Bolton days, but he did not seem to be in the same league as the likes of Colin Bell, Francis Lee or Mike Summerbee. The promising North Manchester youngster Tony Towers wore the number 11 shirt and modestly related later that opponents used to ask him during matches how he managed to get into such a good team! I can't imagine that such comments did his confidence much good.

I asked dad if he could take me to a City game for my twelfth birthday. One of my friends' dads had taken me to watch United against Sheffield United where twenty thousand had been locked out and George Best had taken on the whole Sheffield team before slotting one in at the Scoreboard End. I had also been to see Rochdale take on Luton Town which was memorable for crowd trouble and an early appearance by a left back called Malcolm Macdonald. A third birthday treat involved a James Bond double bill of "Thunderball" and "Doctor No". Dad agreed to take me and three friends to the game against Newcastle United in early October. But things were changing at Maine Road too with the demolishing of the old Scoreboard End, soon to be replaced by the imaginatively titled North Stand. That end of the ground was a building site, and its only occupants were a solitary bulldozer and an occasional bored-looking ball boy. It was really strange watching a game with a crowd on only three sides of the pitch. But the attendances had not fallen. There were very few free seats in the Platt Lane and the Kippax seemed tightly packed.

I was a little disappointed to see the return of two of City's more "combative" players in Dave Connor and George Heslop. The Newcastle side contained such experienced campaigners as Iam McFaul, Frank Clark, Bobby Moncur, Pop Robson and the mighty Wyn Davies. They also included the tricky Norwegian Ben Arentoft at inside left. But alas the game was played out largely in midfield with lots of endeavour but little skill. Nowadays the media would say that both sides cancelled each other out. I hoped that my friends were not too disappointed, but however hard I tried to talk up the match on our way home I felt deep down that we had not made any new converts, and even wondered whether going to see James Bond at the Palace would not have been a safer option. Oh, well. The match finished in a 1-1 draw, Doyle being the City goalscorer. This game seemed to typify City's league form in that they drew more games that season than they won or lost and seemed to settle for a mid-table position. Sure there were highlights, as in the fantastic 4-1 victory at Old Trafford in which Francis Lee scored a hat trick. But even this famous victory was marred by the tragic injury to Glyn Pardoe. His broken leg kept him out for over a year and despite brave comebacks was to effectively end his career. This was bad enough but it was revealed many years later that due to complications setting in, and unknown to Glyn at the time, he nearly lost his leg, and perhaps even his life!

Christmas usually meant a visit to the Pantomine at the Palace in Manchester starring the likes of Ken Dodd, Jack Douglas or Des O'Connor. Apart from the "He is behind you" and "Oh, yes he is" routines there is one particular incident that stood out for me. I remember that half way through the show it was decided to play a game of bingo. We were informed that our cards were below our seats. I scrambled around and sure enough there it was. As the game reached an unlikely crescendo I realised that I only needed one number to win. I could not contain my excitement. Suddenly they announced my number. I screamed "House!" But so did everybody else. You see, all the cards were identical! I have never really understood the popularity of bingo.

On Christmas Day we three boys would usually wake up at some unearthly hour and like children everywhere creep downstairs to see what Santa had brought us. Our presents were usually placed not in a stocking but on our own chair. We were thrilled to get a torch, an Action Man, a castle, a Beano Annual, a selection box or some toy soldiers. But on Christmas day in 1970 I could hardly believe my eyes! A "Subbuteo" football set as my main present! What is more, dad had mounted the green cloth pitch on a sturdy piece of hardboard. It looked like Wembley to me. As soon as I saved up enough money I would go down to Needham and Hesps Sport shop in Middleton to buy a new team of players and it was not long before Manchester City were taking on and beating the likes of Brazil, Holland and Peru!

After Christmas, City ran into a backlog of fixtures and were hit by a succession of injuries to key players. I saw the Blues take on Coventry at Maine Road without Joe Corrigan, Tony Book, Glyn Pardoe, Alan Oakes, and my favourite Mike Summerbee. Their replacements were largely untried youngsters such as Ronnie Healey, Derek Jeffries, Willie Donachie, Tony Towers and Spiderman Ian Mellor. I absolutely adored Mellor because his legs were thinner than mine and he had made it as a professional footballer! (There was still hope for me). The afternoon was grey and drizzly (as always), the attendance only 22000, the pitch very muddy and the lights were on from the start. Coventry wore a fantastic green and black striped kit and contained the likes of Bill Glazier, Mick Coop, and Chris Cattlin who seemed to have always played for them. And yes, the game ended in a 1-1 draw with Francis Lee scoring for us. We sat in the corner of the Platt Lane stand where it joined the Maine Stand, which was becoming a favourite vantage point. Perhaps it was because the benches were actually City blue in colour. Some sections of the stand were painted yellow and maroon harking back to previous away strips. There was even a green section! Surely the whole stand would have looked better in blue? Perhaps they did not have enough paint.

Although City had been knocked out of both domestic cups relatively early they were again making a strong challenge in the European Cup Winners Cup. Having entered as Cup holders they brushed aside Linfield and Honved before incredibly being drawn once again with the Polish side Gornik. It is a credit to the ability of these City youngsters that in those far off days of wafer thin first team squads that the Blues not only retained a respectable place in the table, but also managed to overcome the mighty Gornik after taking them to a third game in neutral Copenhagen where we ran out victors by three goals to one. It almost goes without saying that this wonderful evening in Copenhagen was not televised. A crackly radio and the Daily Express was all that we had back in the early Seventies!

City finally ran out of steam in the semi final against Chelsea losing by a single goal at both Maine Road and at Stamford Bridge. It had been a strange season in many ways. Not only was the structure of the ground changing before our eyes, but there were many dramas being played out behind the scenes that had little interest for a football mad twelve year old, but must have had some effect on events on the pitch. I am referring to the proposed takeover in the boardroom which eventually resulted in the removal of Albert Alexander as Chairman and the emergence of a certain Peter Swales. The funniest lines attributed to little Albert that I have heard was when he went into the dressing rooms to congratulate the team on their promotion to Division 1 in 1966 and said "Well done everybody. Now we will make lots of money and will be able to go out and buy some good players." Fantastic!

More upsetting to the majority of City fans and certainly to the players was the rift that was beginning to emerge between the two men that had made all this success possible-Joe Mercer and Malcolm Allison. Big Mal later claimed that Joe had said to him back in 1965 that he would be happy to hand over the reins as Manager after two years. But clearly after year on year success there was no way that anyone would do such a thing, and anyway it was obvious to every body, especially to the players, that it was the partnership of Joe and Mal that was the key. Malcolm was frustrated in his desire to be number one and became a prime mover in forcing through the boardroom takeover with Joe on the opposite side resistant to change. All of this made the front and back pages of the papers and to be honest left me cold at the time. It was all too grown up and boring like politics and the News, and not for me. In fact I attended fewer matches that season than before or since.

At the beginning of season 1971-72 there was great optimism in the air at Maine Road. The new North Stand terrace with its electronic scoreboard was ready for the first match. A major addition to the playing staff was the signing of centre forward Wyn Davies from Newcastle United. Wyn was played up front as a target man, which set free Francis Lee to have the season of his life. With Mike Summerbee on the right and "spider" Mellor on the left there was a regular supply of crosses onto the head of Wyn which he would nod down for Frannie to finish off. Francis scored an unbelievable 33 League goals that season including 13 penalties which prompted the rumour that City had signed a Chinaman some thirty years before Sun Jihai made his debut. And this fellow's name. Lee Won Pen.

City swept all before them at Maine Road with high scoring wins against Crystal Palace, Tottenham, Southampton, Coventry and Ipswich, and took part in the scintillating November derby against United which ended in a 3-3 draw. By February 1972 City were top of the league two points ahead of Leeds and Derby and three points ahead of United. It was then that grandad Keogh asked me if I would like to go over to Sheffield for a weekend to stay at Auntie Eileens' with himself and grandma. Dad

41

came from a typical Catholic family of that time in that he had two brothers Mike and John, three sisters Eileen, Margaret and Maureen, and very little money. I thought a visit to Eileens' was a strange request, as this was certainly not the sort of thing we did as a family. But when he added that we would be going to watch City play Sheffield United at Bramall Lane I could not believe my ears. My first away game! (I did not include Old Trafford).

Grandad had by now recently retired from his job as a street cleaner for the council. We regularly used to arrive home from school to find his green van outside our house where he was probably having a crafty brew! He did not own a car so we took the train from Manchester Piccadilly over the Pennines to be met on the platform by dad's sister Eileen. I really liked Eileen partly because she seemed to have such a sunny disposition, but also out of respect for the fact that she had really struck out on her own. She had gone to University in the fifties when girls from such a humble background as hers in North Manchester did not do. She graduated, became a teacher, married an actor, and moved to Sheffield! She was also my godmother so she had a special place in my affections. I was so excited about going to the match but first had to negotiate an unsettling Friday evening. Grandad, Eileen and her husband went out to the local pub leaving me with grandma. What on earth would we talk about, as she had absolutely no interest in football? That night without any prompting she totally opened her heart to me, a gawky 13 year old with little experience of life. She told me all about her heartbreak when she was told years earlier that she would be giving birth to a disabled daughter, our auntie Maureen. She went into medical detail that I did not really understand and I did not have the words to convey my feelings. I did know that what she was telling me was incredibly important to her. But as I did not have the words for such a conversation I decided that it would be best to simply listen. Many years later Eileen told me that it would have been an extremely unusual thing for grandma to have spoken in this way, and it is only now that I feel rather privileged that she chose to do so.

I opened my curtains and was thrilled to be able to see the floodlights from my window. At breakfast I was informed that they were those of Sheffield Wednesday and not Sheffield United. We caught a bus into the town centre and walked to the ground nervously chattering in anticipation of this top of the table clash. As we entered the turnstile I bought the programme "Lane Line Up" for the mighty sum of 6p. Adverts told us that we could drive away in a Vauxhall Viva for £801-87, make the match with the drinking man's drink Watney Bitter, and travel to Anfield for 80p. I was heartened to read that Sheffield United had lost their last home game 5-0 to Arsenal, and amazed that Malcolm Allison, now officially team manager, was predicting that City would win at least six trophies in the next ten years. We took up our position in front of a crush barrier (for my protection) by the players tunnel on the half way line amongst a group of friendly middle aged Yorkshiremen. As I looked across I was amazed to see that there was no stand on the opposite touchline. You see, Bramall Lane still doubled up as Yorkshire County Cricket Club in the summer, and through a ghostly mist beyond the T.V. gantry I could just make out the cricket pavilion on the far side of the field.

Sheffield United were a decent side containing stalwarts such as Len Badger, Eddie Colquhoun and Alan Woodward, the mercurial Tony Currie who should have played many more times for England, and of course Trevor Hockey who looked like a cross between Roy Wood of Wizzard and the American Werewolf in London. City included Willie Donachie a young Scottish full back who had made the number 3 shirt his own and Tony Towers who had reclaimed the number 11 shirt from Ian Mellor. I was dismayed that Neil Young had been transferred from the club. He seemed to have been too easily dispensed with after all his spectacular goals and years of marvellous service. It does seem that everything was either black or white with Malcolm and you were either in or out. Neil spent a short spell with Preston before moving on to Rochdale, where he found it soul destroying that when he went over to take a corner he could hear the buses passing by outside the ground. And this was only a short time after playing in front of full houses of 60000 at Old Trafford, Anfield and Highbury.

The game at Bramall Lane was fast and furious and swung from end to end with Francis Lee in terrific form and Colin Bell making those trademark late runs into the box. Trevor Hockey was breathing fire and kicking everything that moved. Both sides were awarded penalties and scored from them. A draw was the fairest result and both teams left the field to a standing ovation after it ended 3-3. I watched the game again on Match of The Day before making the journey back home on the train to Manchester the next afternoon. It had been a momentous weekend!

As the excitement increased at the top of the table there were four teams in with a real shout for the title including City. My visits to Maine Road were becoming more regular. March began with victories over West Brom, Arsenal and Everton and with the Blues poised on the brink with ten games to go Malcolm made a decision, which was to send shockwaves

44

through the club and in my view cost City the Championship. There is an old adage in football that says, "Never change a winning team". And this is just what Malcolm did when he signed Rodney Marsh from QPR and thrust him straight into the side. On his debut against Chelsea it was clear that Rodney was used to a different style of play to that of City. City played a fast direct game based on the simple formula of pass and move. Thus when a player received the ball his team mates would be immediately on the move giving him three or four options. When Rodney received the ball he preferred to slow the game down, have a look around and only then release the ball. This caused team mates to stop their runs allowing defenders to regroup and mark their opponents. Unfortunately Rodney was also overweight and seemed unfit to the casual observer. Surely Malcolm Allison could see what everybody else could see and he should have been told to leave Rodney out of the side until the start of the next season when all being well City would have been the Champions of England once again. But Malcolm had a huge ego and wanted things done his way. Tony Towers made way for Rodney.

City did beat Chelsea 1-0 but after a goalless draw against Newcastle were due to face mid table Stoke City on April Fools Day at Maine Road. That was the day that goalkeeper Gordon Banks, now coming towards the end of a glorious career, took on Man City on his own. On a wet blustery day with treacherous conditions in the goalmouths Gordon gave the finest display of goalkeeping that I have ever seen from a visiting keeper. Some of the saves he made from Francis Lee in particular down at the Platt Lane end in front of dad and I were simply out of this world. I vividly remember Francis on his knees on the pitch beating the ground in frustration. The second half was all one-way traffic but Stoke hung on grimly to defeat City by two goals to one. As we trudged back to the car, in our new parking spot just off Platt Lane, I was full of hope but dad said nothing. He knew that the title race was over for the Blues. Dad did not speak when there was no need to do so. His silence often speaking louder than words.

A further defeat at Southampton prompted Malcolm to finally drop Rodney to the bench for the Manchester derby at Old Trafford, but it could be argued that the damage had already been done as his inclusion had disrupted the fluid City style of play. He came on late in the game to score City's third goal to maintain their fantastic run of five successive League victories at Old Trafford.

Everything should have been set up for the final match of the season on the 22nd of April 1972 against league leaders Derby County. Unfortunately for the Blues the title was out of our hands. Even though this was our last match Derby, Liverpool, and Leeds had not completed their fixtures so we had to rely on other teams beating them. This was very disappointing as only a few weeks earlier the Blues had been points clear at the top.

The programme indicated that Joe Mercer was still the manager but that Malcolm Allison was the new "team" manager. A strange set of affairs where even Joe did not know what his role was. Elsewhere in the programme it stated that a coach could take you from Manchester to Hampden Park in Glasgow for £3-80 including lunch and a match ticket to the International against Scotland. If you played "City bingo" you could win prizes from 20p to £1 each week, and you could watch Top Class Comedy Duo Cannon and Ball at the Social Club.

Derby County were an excellent side managed by Brian Clough and Peter Taylor and contained the likes of Roy Mcfarland, Colin Todd, Archie Gemmill, Kevin Hector, and white-booted winger Alan Hinton. This was a rare all-ticket match for the seats and mine costing 25p was on row 38 in Block B3 in the Platt Lane stand. This was a game in which Rodney really did turn on the style. There was no doubt that he was an extremely gifted footballer. He was simply not the right man for City at that particular time in March 1972. Nevertheless he scored a fantastic goal at the Platt Lane End drifting in from the right past two or three defenders before slotting the ball past Colin Boulton. Francis Lee scored the other goal to round off a vintage display from the Blues. Interestingly, Wyn Davies did not appear in this game and would be sold on early the next season to arch rivals Man United. All City could do was to wait for the other sides to complete their fixtures. Agonisingly Derby won their final game to take the Championship with City finishing fourth on goal difference but only one point behind! So near and yet so far.

FOUR.

GROUND CONTROL TO MAJOR RON.

I was by now a fully-fledged teenager. Like most others my thoughts were turning towards music, fashion and girls, in no particular order. My order of Shoot from the corner shop was now replaced by a serious addiction to New Musical Express, Sounds and Melody Maker. While groups such as Slade, T Rex, Sweet, and Mud were vying with heartthrobs like Donny Osmond, David Cassidy and the Bay City Rollers at the top of the pop charts, more progressive friends at school had lots of hair and were seriously into Led Zeppelin and Yes. Brother Pete was starting to lose interest in football, but he was very cool where music was concerned. He started a lifetime obsession with David Bowie, who we had recently caught on "Lift Off with Ayshea" singing "Starman". As soon as the LP "Ziggy Stardust" was released it was never off our turntable, and I shared Pete's admiration for singles like "John, I'm only dancing" and "Drive-in Saturday". I would cycle around the streets of Middleton with my transistor radio precariously suspended from the handlebars of my second-hand racing bike belting out the Top Twenty to the bemusement of passers by. Glam rock was in vogue and particular favourites were "Get it On" by T Rex, "Virginia Plain" by Roxy Music and the fantastic "This town ain't big enough for the both of us" by Sparks who had Hitler on keyboards. Thursday night belonged to Top Of The Pops and we taped the charts on "Boots" cassettes on Sunday evenings.

How one looked to the opposite sex was becoming very important. Up until now mum and dad bought all our clothes and we had little say in the matter. I remember Pete and I being verbally abused by a local thug, whose name was on every wall on the estate, as we warily made our way up the road in our new Sunday best of matching paisley shirt and tie complemented by crimplene trousers. I think he actually questioned our sexuality. Anyway things began to change for the better on the fashion front as mum began to trust us to buy some of our own gear. Armed with "spends" I gingerly made my way through the skinheads, suedeheads and perry boys to Stolen From Ivor in the market centre in Manchester and bought a yellow jumper, blue Ben Sherman shirt, and unbelievable purple and blue two-tone trousers. Even though by now I was approaching six foot tall I also managed to get some purple six-inch platform shoes which incredibly I wore to school! The hard men around town at this time wore Crombie coats, turned up jeans, red socks and Doc Martin "bovver" boots. "Clockwork Orange" was released that year amid much controversy, although there was no chance of me getting in to the local cinema to see such a violent "X" film. Those that did so told me that the uniform worn by the gangs included bowler hats, white coats, and make up. I never saw any bowler hats or make up but certainly the white coats did make an appearance on the terraces in the mid-seventies. I remember on one occasion being chased through the town centre of Burnley by a gang wearing white butcher's coats!

Living in an all male family (sorry mum), and going to an all boys school made the business of meeting girls seem like something from another universe. It just did not happen. Or not to me anyway. It soon began to be a matter of life and death to me which bus I would be able to catch home at night after school. You see I had to time it so that the coach from the Girls Grammar School would arrive at the same time and unload its charges onto the streets of Middleton. There was one girl in particular with whom I became infatuated, and I would walk night after night on the other side of the road from her until she disappeared into her house just after the roundabout, before I turned right at the crossroads into my street. If I got off the bus and she was there my heart missed a beat and how I avoided trees and lampposts I do not know, as I followed in a haze bewitched by her brown uniform as winter turned to spring. However if the bus and coach did not coincide as was often the case, and she was not there, then I walked home with a heavy heart like a character from "Doctor Zhivago". This went on for about a year, I guess. I never spoke to her, not even to ask her name. That would have been impossible.

City began season 1972-73 with six defeats from the first eight matches. Brother Pete was by now fixated with Ziggy Stardust and his Spiders from Mars, and Maine Road had ceased to be an attraction. But on September 16th 1972 Dad and I were joined by youngest brother Paul, who now aged 8 was deemed old enough to join our crusade. By some strange coincidence our opponents that day for his first game were Tottenham Hotspur! But there the similarity between our first games ended. The sun was shining brightly as Paul gasped as he reached the top of the Platt Lane stairs and saw the green carpet stretched out in front of him. At the other end the North Stand had been filled with green tip-up seats (far-removed from the traditional benches) reducing the stadium capacity and leaving only the Kippax as a standing area, which was very rare for the time. With

51

the sun on their backs the Blues hit form, and with two goals from Rodney Marsh defeated Spurs 2-1. The crowd sang his praises to the tune of "Son of my father", this being the one-hit wonder for Chicory Tip. The sunshine, the optimism and the slick performance that greeted Paul that day were all absent on my debut six years earlier. In typical City fashion though, they went down 5-1 to Stoke the following week.

At this stage I guess you could call us regulars as we were attending most home games. We witnessed a pulsating Third Round cup tie in which City beat Stoke by the odd goal in five, only for the Blues to be drawn against Liverpool at Anfield. The Blues escaped with a goalless draw to force a replay the following Wednesday. That night the atmosphere was incredible with fans tightly crammed like sardines in the Kippax. Overhead electric bulbs being blown in the wind were creating a dance hall effect on the swaying masses below. Needless to say it had rained all day creating a greasy top surface. Colin Bell and Tommy Booth were the goal scorers as City sent mighty Liverpool back down the East Lancs Road with their tales between their legs. The excitement was building and in school our transistor radios were tuned in to the F.A. Cup Fifth Round draw which paired City against Sunderland, which was to take place on Saturday the 24th of February. We were delighted as we saw this as almost a bye into the next round as Sunderland were in the Second Division. Could this really be our year?

The match programme reminded us that the highest aggregate attendances in the First Division were at Manchester United, Liverpool, and Arsenal, with City in sixth place. The leading goal scorers were Brian "Pop" Robson of West Ham, John Richards of Wolves, Malcolm

Macdonald of Newcastle, and Alan "Sniffer" Clarke of Leeds. Needless to say that all sixteen names in this list, including Rodney Marsh, were born in the British Isles. It was still some years before Ardiles and Villa began the influx of foreign players to our game. Adverts included one for Peter J. Swales Ltd. inviting one and all to "see his famous selection of £1 handbags", and others such as Mike Doyle's Hartshead Motors and Colin Bell's Restaurant showed that the players needed to branch out to seek their fortune.

With our pink tickets (30p for Juniors) clutched tightly in our hands dad, Paul and I took up our places behind the goal to await the slaughter. City were at full strength and Sunderland contained three future Blues in Dave Watson, Dennis Tueart and Mick Horswill and others such as Jim Montgomery and Ian Porterfield who were soon to become household names. I have never seen the Kippax so tightly packed, as it was that day with 55000 in the ground. There were a lot of Red and White scarves around the ground. Sunderland had a superb following and I think that there were a number of United fans inside Maine Road as their game had been called off earlier in the day.

The first half was all one way traffic as City with a goal from Tony Towers were steamrollering their way to Wembley. And then it happened. For no apparent reason Joe Corrigan passed the ball straight to Mick Horswill who gleefully accepted the gift and duly equalised. The sheer power seemed to slip out of City's play. The game ended in a two-all draw, and on a famous night on Wearside in front of a huge television audience City were defeated 3-1 in the replay. At fourteen years of age this was a bitter pill to swallow. I was convinced that this was our year, but it was not to be. In that now famous Final Sunderland manager Bob Stokoe danced across the Wembley turf in his trilby hat to embrace goalkeeping hero Jim Montgomery as they overcame mighty Leeds with a goal from Ian Porterfield. It should have been Big Mal running to congratulate Joe Corrigan!

After the Sunderland defeat City lost five of their next six games, and although recovering to reach eleventh place the season ended on a very flat note, and I for the first time in my life was glad to see the back of football for a few weeks. Malcolm Allison must have had similar thoughts to me as he left Maine Road to join Crystal Palace. He made noises about being dissatisfied with the Board over the selling of Ian Mellor to Norwich, but I am sure that deep down he knew that he had made some bad decisions, in particular within his relationship with Joe Mercer who had by now left City for Coventry, and of course with the signing of Rodney Marsh.

1973 was the year that colour came into our lives in a big way. The Granada TV Rentals van outside our house as I arrived home could mean only one thing. We were getting our first colour television set! We could not contain our excitement! The air had not been so electric since dad knocked down the gatepost. If not before, then we certainly became "telly addicts" from that day onwards. On Saturday nights we had to sit through the Val Doonican or Nana Mouskouri show while we waited for "Match of the Day". We could now watch Liverpool against Chelsea and see Red against Blue rather than Grey against Grey. We completed our homework in time to fall in love with Jenny Agutter in "The Railway Children", say good night to Johnboy in "The Waltons", try to break out of "Colditz", and explore the delights of Batley and Castleford in floodlit Rugby League with the great Eddie Waring. At first some of the pictures had a ghostly outline in red, yellow and green. I don't know if this was due to the technology of the time or our particular set, but we did not let it spoil our enjoyment.

There were so many great comedy shows on TV at that time. Our favourites included "Porridge", "Some Mothers Do Have 'Em", "Dad's Army" and "The Likely Lads", which have been repeated numerous times since. Others would probably struggle to get a showing today like "Till Death Us Do Part", "Up Pompeii", and Benny Hill as tastes have become far more politically correct. I absolutely adored "Steptoe and Son" but dad was not keen on us watching it due to the bad language, which was extremely rare on the BBC in the early seventies. We were sent up to bed because of this but used to sit on the stairs somewhat confused to hear mum and dad in hysterics at events on Oil Drum Lane, Shepherds Bush. One programme that we could all sit down together and watch was the fantastic "Morecambe and Wise show". They were absolute gods. Eric was of course a Director of Luton Town and he took every possible opportunity to give them a plug.

Dad was very Catholic and would not have anything on TV that he thought was mocking the Church. Therefore we were well into our teens before we could really appreciate the comedian Dave Allen. (Although if dad was out at the pub then mum did allow us to watch. Thanks mum.) One programme that was only short lived but did make it onto our screen for several minutes was a comedy entitled "Me Mammy". It seemed a harmless jibe at Irish Catholics, but when they produced a board game entitled "Popeopoly" dad hit the roof and that was that!

The summer holidays brought the new delights of "Children's T.V." where we were entertained by black and white classics such as the dubbed "Flashing Blade", "Belle and Sebastian", "The White Horses", and of course "Robinson Crusoe". I can still hear the parrot squawking " Poor Robinson". We also enjoyed the bizarre "Clangers", and of course "The Banana Splits" which had a great signature tune, which did not take long to be adapted for use on the terraces. "Manchester la, la, la, Manchester la, la, la."

In choosing their new manager the Blues turned to their backroom staff by appointing Johnny Hart who had served the club with some distinction in a variety of roles since the Fifties. His first act raised many eyebrows in Manchester as he sensationally signed Denis Law from United. Although Denis was coming to the end of a magnificent career this was nevertheless a major coup. Transfers between the two clubs have been few and far between over the years but Denis was so highly respected that he was welcomed by all Blues. It may have helped that he had played for City early on in his career and memorably scored six in one match against Luton Town in a game that was later abandoned! Denis did not disappoint by scoring two on his debut against Birmingham City, but I am afraid to say that I missed it due to our annual family holiday, which that year took us to distant Scarborough.

City were beginning to turn on the style at home with their "Fantasy League" forward line of Summerbee, Bell, Lee, Law and Marsh. Also Glyn Pardoe was recovering from his horrific injury against United and getting a run in the side. Unfortunately big Joe Corrigan was starting to come under pressure and suffering abuse from some of City's notoriously critical "fans". After a heavy defeat at Burnley the Blues signed a new keeper Keith MacRae from Motherwell. My first sighting of him came in the visit of Arsenal on November 10th in which a further new signing Mick Lester made his debut. My first impressions of ginger haired MacRae were that he was a good shot stopper, but that he was too slight and did not really command his goal area. He didn't that day as City slipped to a rare home defeat. And as for Mick Lester, well his debut turned out to be his only full appearance in four years with the club. That game was also notable in that it was the first time that I had felt frightened at a football match. Hooliganism was taking a hold on English football but thankfully there was very little seen at Maine Road. But at three-quarter time that day when the gates opened to let people out, a hundred or more City "fans" swept into the Platt Lane Stand looking for a fight with the few Arsenal fans scattered around. Dad reassured me that everything was OK and order was duly restored.

Sadly all was not well behind the scenes with manager Hart unable to cope with the stresses and strains of managing City and after only six months in charge he resigned. His replacement was "Sergeant Major" Ron Saunders who seemed at the time to be the wrong choice in that he did not appear to fit the "City" mould and seemed totally ill suited to deal with the likes of Lee, Summerbee, Marsh and Law who were some of the greatest characters in the game. The fact that he was so publicly backed by fledgling chairman Peter Swales was, with hindsight, ominous. In fact Swales nailed his colours to the mast in December programme notes by stating that when Saunders goes then so does Swales. Saunders left six months later, only to be followed by Peter Swales......... in 1994.

At school the beatings continued, and I managed to avoid the majority of them. I was occasionally strapped for the heinous crimes of grinning or turning round. There was one teacher who we all feared who took the weekly Technical Drawing class, and was generally known as "Bully". Very few of us slept the night before his lessons. At the beginning of each lesson he reminded us that he did not like children and that he used to work in industry. He then proceeded to hand out immaculately sharpened pencils. If any of us had the misfortune to allow our pencil to hit the floor and damage one of the leads "that he had sharpened to perfection", then it was an immediate fine or if we had no money then it was a thrashing. I do not use the term loosely. This was not the worst crime that you could commit in his class. The worst thing you could do was to yawn. It was widely known that if you yawned he paraded you out to the front of the class. He then asked you if you yawned because you were tired or bored. If you said that you were bored then you got six of the best. If you had the "temerity" to say that you were tired then older boys told us that he filled the huge sink with water and proceeded to dunk you in it over and over, while reminding everybody of your general worthlessness. I guess that some boys were tired because, like me, they had hardly slept the night before. Needless to say, very few boys continued with Tech Drawing at the end of the year.

New Years Day was memorable for reasons of a "family outing" to watch City against Stoke. What was highly unusual was that Dad, Paul, and I were joined by both grandad and aunty Margaret for this match. And what is more we stood on the terraces in the corner of the Kippax down by the corner flag at the Platt Lane end. I guess that this must have been because this is where grandad and Margaret used to stand together in the fifties watching names like Revie, Trautmann, Hayes, Paul, Ewing, Clarke and Johnny Hart. I listened enraptured by this talk of an earlier era, but could only imagine a teenaged aunty Margaret with her dark haired handsome father making fortnightly trips to watch the 56 Cup winners on some kind of grainy newsreel with piano accompaniment. Anyway this particular game against Stoke was largely forgettable ending in a goalless draw. Yet what I cannot forget is the way that Margaret remonstrated fiercely with men around us who were abusing City goalkeeper Joe Corrigan, (who had been recalled to the side), throughout the afternoon. She told them in no uncertain terms that they could not call themselves true City fans. And what is more she silenced them.

Early 1974 was a traumatic time not only for City but for the country as a whole. There was a power crisis and the lights would literally go out at any time. We had to stock up with candles and Swan Vesta matches and our torches that we received a couple of Christmases ago proved indispensable. There was a three-day working week as great industrial unrest swept the nation. As far as I was concerned I wondered how football would be affected and the first sign appeared in the programme against Leicester on January 12th apologising for the reduced nature of the Match Magazine. Perhaps more crucially, due to the fact that floodlights could not be used there would be an afternoon kick off in a couple of weeks for the cup replay against Coventry. This would surely hit the attendance including myself as there would be no way that mum and dad would allow me to miss school!

That Saturday lunchtime Dad arrived home from shopping as I was slumped in front of the television watching "Football Focus" which was in my opinion far superior to ITV's offering of "On The Ball". "Get your coat on son, we'll just make kick off if we get our skates on", said dad to my absolute amazement and delight. Improvisation was not his strongest subject. But we made it just in time. We were so on the last minute that instead of entering the Platt Lane Stand via the solitary turnstile inside the Kippax as we usually did, we made our way right into the centre of the Kippax and stood on the half way line about a dozen rows from the front. What an amazing view! You could almost touch your heroes, and it felt as if I was running the line! This was so different from what I was used to. We were surrounded by hard, working men. You could smell the beer, nicotine, sweat and tears.

Dad sensed my unease, but as the game started I relaxed, absorbed in the contest between City's five-star attack and Leicester's hard man defence which included Steve Whitworth, Dennis Rofe, Malcolm Munro and Graham Cross backed by the excellent Peter Shilton. Even a side such as Leicester who were perennially fighting relegation contained brilliant individuals like Keith Weller, Alan Birchenall and Frank Worthington; such was the nature of the First Division in the early seventies. It was a hard fought victory, which City won with goals from Rodney Marsh and Denis Law. If anybody fancied a weekend away in 1974 the diminished programme invited you to spend a mini holiday in London comprising second-class train travel and bed and breakfast in a city centre hotel for the princely sum of just £8-50!

I really milked this unexpected visit to Maine Road when I went to school on Monday. I impressed my friends, who had as little experience of the world as me, by telling them how I had stood alongside some of the hardest men in Manchester, and talked with them about their exploits of terrace battles with opposing fans. I am sure that my classmates thought that I had consumed ten Players No6 and two or three Double Diamonds at half-time!

Two days later City had to get past Coventry in order to reach the League Cup semi final. This was the match that was to take place at two o'clock in the afternoon due to the power crisis. We all took our transistor radios into class, none of which had earpieces of any kind. So it was a case of hiding them in our desks with the volume turned down very low. We relied on our classmates to create a general hubbub of conversation, which would provide enough cover for us to listen to the match. The first half passed off well in that the teacher was so weak that we could have listened to the game with the volume on full blast. It helped that there was not much to cheer about with City losing 2-1 for long periods.

We were all looking forward to the second half as our next teacher was even weaker than the previous one, but horror of horrors, he chose that day to contract flu, and as the door swung open the most terrifying and mean spirited teacher in the school made his not so grand entrance. There was no chance of keeping up with the score at this rate. Nevertheless "Carrot" who sat near the front was fearless and heralded City's equaliser with a muted yelp, which broke the silence. The class erupted in laughter, the Blues were elated and Carrot earned himself a detention. Carrot lived on the other side of the tracks to myself and my "wet" compatriots. He was duly nicknamed not because of the colour of his hair but for his protruding teeth. In fact he was a dead ringer for Freddy Mercury! They say that children can be cruel, but Grammar school boys? He used to be absent every Thursday and it transpired he ran a market stall in South Manchester. For the record, after equalising City went on to win 4-2 with a late show of style and grace missing from too many performances that season. I went home not even caring if the Girls Grammar School bus was due, as I was looking forward to watching the highlights that night on TV, and once again I was starting to make preparations for a Wembley visit.

Only lowly Plymouth Argyle stood between City and another major Cup Final. But the difference with this one was that mum and dad said that if they get through then I would be able to go! A one-all draw in another afternoon kick-off brought both teams back to Maine Road with City strong favourites to get through to Wembley. For some reason this game was played at night under floodlights.

Amazingly I was allowed to go with my friends from school. Best mate Macker who sat alongside me in lessons was City daft, his dad coming from Moss Side when it was really quite an attractive area, as he regularly reminded us. In fact, he went to school with ex-Red Denis Viollet. We caught the bus at the end of Kingsway which took us into Manchester, where we met Dave Moore and the three of us walked across to Aytoun Street where we got the number 76 Match Bus from opposite the old Grand Hotel. As we excitedly jumped off the bus and followed the crowd along the familiar narrow terrace streets the heavens opened and it threw it down. It was always like this! We entered the ground by the first Kippax Street turnstile where it joined the North Stand, bought a programme, and not having the courage to go into the centre of the stand ran to our right and stood in the same corner where I had watched my first Derby with Dad some seven years ago.

Plymouth contained a young Paul Mariner in their side who was to go on to play many games for Ipswich, Arsenal and England. But City were not in the mood for any favours and ruthlessly swept aside the opposition with goals from Colin Bell and Francis Lee to win 2-0 and reach Wembley where they would face Wolverhampton Wanderers.

FIVE.

A BACK HEEL FROM DENIS.

Dad had two brothers, John and Mike, and while both being really nice guys they seemed like chalk and cheese when compared with each other. John the elder was pretty quiet yet had a dry sense of humour. We really admired him as he had done some serious acting and had even appeared in "Coronation Street" and "Crown Court". Only a couple of years earlier he had had a major part in the serial "Family At War" and had brought actors home to grandmas for tea! He did not really speak to us much about football, and my main memory of John is going to his wedding in Buxton crammed like sardines into a motorbike and sidecar. After two hours of going up and down every hill in Derbyshire I was as sick as a dog when we arrived.

Uncle Mike was many years younger than dad (in fact he was nearer my age) and we loved him because he always played soccer and Subbuteo football with the three of us. He was a really outgoing character, and I remember him once calling at our house on the way back from the hippy trail to Marrakesh. I did not recognise him with a full beard and clad in an Arab cape and sandals. Not the usual outfit for a night out in Middleton! On Saturdays he would turn out for Middleton Amateurs on the local recreation ground and according to grandad it was a very high standard of football that they played. The fact that they had netting in the goals and had real referees dressed in black seemed to confirm this. I was very much looking forward to seeing Uncle Mike play in the local derby and arranged to meet grandad on the touchline. It was ten to three as I scampered through Middleton town centre and I was quite out of breath as I joined him and eagerly scanned the field for my favourite uncle. " I thought he played at the back, grandad?" I enquired as I looked carefully at each blue shirted figure. Grandad had a strange look on his face as he sorrowfully declared that Uncle Mike had been sent off for violent conduct in the first minute of the game. When he appeared on the line a few minutes later he greeted me with an unaccustomed embarrassed look on his face. Grandad remained stonily silent for the rest of the afternoon.

To my surprise many years later I was talking at the bar in a Middleton hostelry to a Moonraker (Middletonian) of long standing. When he asked my name and I replied Keogh, he enquired if I was related to John Keogh. "He scored the best goal I have ever seen in my life. I used to be a goalkeeper. While playing for St. Peters in the Fifties I threw the ball out to Keogh who was standing just inside our half of the field. He jinked inside two opponents before letting fly from fully fifty yards. The goalie never even moved. The ball screamed into the top corner! What a goal!" Uncle John had never mentioned any of this to us. He just smiled knowingly, whenever we talked about football.

March 2nd 1974. The day of the League Cup Final. I was awakened from a fitful sleep by dad at the unearthly hour of 5.30am. I was to meet up with one of the older lads off the estate, Chris Finn and his dad, to catch a coach that would leave Middleton Bus Station at seven o'clock for Wembley. I soon located them among the crowds that were thronging Middleton centre bedecked in silk scarves, rosettes and bobble hats, most of whom were clutching duffle bags containing provisions for the day. In my excitement I noticed that I had forgotten my sandwiches which mum had dutifully prepared for me the night before! Then as if on a white charger dad appeared clutching the aforesaid pack of "butties" which he handed to me before wishing me luck. There were butterflies in my stomach as I waved goodbye. I guess I was a little embarrassed that he was waving me off, but at least I had got my sandwiches. I opened the first one within five minutes. How far away was London? I had no idea, as the fleet of some twenty coaches left the safety of Middleton before heading for the M62 and M6 South. It was a huge adventure alighting at a Motorway service station joining the hundreds of excited City fans queuing for a bacon butty and coffee. These were days before football coaches were banned from the services or at least had to make appointments in order to avoid disturbances with other fans. Some five or six hours later we were approaching the outskirts of London, and I got my first sight of Wembley on the hill. Like a cross between the Sacre-Coeur and the Taj Mahal the twin towers were bathed in spring sunshine.

We parked in the huge coach park at the bottom of Wembley Way, and without dad by my side, my immediate worry was that I would not be able to find the coach afterwards. One coach looks like another, and there were hundreds here! I was so proud as City and Wolves fans walked side by side along the road as we re-enacted all those Cup Final customs that I had watched on TV year after year. Suddenly a huge roar rang out as the team coach inched past us! Past the hot dog stands, the rosette sellers and the man in a flat cap with a board reminding us that the world would end very soon I reached the top of Wembley Way. I turned to watch a sea of Sky Blue and Old Gold inching its way up the hill. We entered the turnstiles together at the tunnel end, but I had to stand in a different section to Chris and his dad as the stand was divided into small pens. We were so early that I was able to make my way right down to the front. Minutes later one of City's more famous supporters "Big Helen", who sold flowers outside Manchester Royal, announced her arrival in a loud voice only a decibel or two quieter than her notorious bell. With a small crowd of children in her wake, like the Pied Piper of Ancoats, she took up her position behind the goal only yards away from me. There were still two hours to kick off!

My match ticket cost 80 pence, and I bought a programme for the princely sum of 15 pence. It was packed with colour pictures which was very unusual for the time and contained full page adverts for Pale Ale which "works wonders," cigars which "make a good time great," and Player's No6 cigarettes which were the "most popular filter cigarette in Britain." In health-conscious Britain in 1974 I guess you could say that adverts were clearly aimed at the working man, and not at a family audience. Inside the programme was the free League Football magazine, which was a little bit more up-market by including adverts for whisky! The colour action photos in the programme show Tommy Booth in both penalty areas (he was here, there, and every flippin' where, in those days!), and what is remarkable is that every single teenager behind the goals is wearing a green parka with a red hood!

Being behind the goals at Wembley meant that you were quite some distance from the pitch due to the dog track. It was also used for Speedway and even the Horse of the Year show! Time passed slowly as I read my programme from back to front largely to a background of the hum of a filling stadium, the occasional chant, the Massed Band of the Royal Engineers, the barks of the RAF police dog demonstration team and the final of the "On the Ball" Penalty Prize Competition. At last the two teams emerged from the tunnel just to my right to an almighty roar! They walked over to the half way line to be presented to the Duke of Kent. I turned round briefly and looked up at the sea of blue and white behind me in the spring sunshine. This was perfect. As good as it gets. And it was. City were clear favourites with their all-star forward line of Summerbee, Bell, Lee, Law, and Marsh pitted against such stalwarts as Derek Parkin, Mike Bailey, Frank Munro and John McAlle. Wolves of course had the great Derek Dougan of Northern Ireland and pancho moustache, along with his young deputy John Richards, who were served by ex Blue David Wagstaffe from the left wing. But surely Doyley and Tommy Booth would easily contain them? The first half passed in a haze of colour and noise, but just before the whistle Kenny Hibbitt put Wolves ahead down at our end of the ground. There was an eerie milli-second of total silence before the opposite end erupted in a crescendo of noise. One nil down at the break. Surely no problem. After all, this was a perfect day.

The Blues trotted out, their studs clattering on the concrete in the tunnel calling to mind the entrance to the field back home. City began to attack our end with a wave of great attacking skill. Eventually Colin Bell (who else?) rounded off a great move to score with aplomb from just inside the area. The crowd went mad. I was hugged by huge beery males and pulled up and down the terracing before resting two rows down nearer the front. City continued to attack but could not finish the Wolves off, whose stand in keeper Pierce was having the game of his life. It was obviously his perfect day, and not mine. Only minutes before the end the ball went upfield, was crossed into the centre, and sucked into the net via John Richards by the huge throng of Wolves fans at the far end. The whistle went soon after. We had lost. For a few seconds I felt numb as younger children began to cry before being comforted by their dads. I felt very alone in a crowd of one hundred thousand. But what was this? Rodney Marsh was walking towards us all and off the pitch with his head down, instead of going up for his losers' tankard with the rest of the team. I knew straight away that this was the wrong thing to do, and an immature response from such a popular player. I felt that this was just another indication that he just did not fit in, and was not right for City. We had to swallow our disappointment and gave the team a rousing reception as they walked slowly down to us before disappearing into the tunnel. Incredibly I found my coach among the hundreds on the coach park. There was a bit of nasty banter between the two sets of fans but nothing major as we waited for nearly two hours before being able to actually get off the park and begin our long journey home. At times on the journey as we sped past places with unheard of names like Milton Keynes and Newport Pagnall, I longed to be at home in front of the fire. I re-read the programme over and over again, and with my enthusiasm returning somewhere near Stoke I actually made plans to go to an away game on my own!

Hooliganism was in full swing in the mid-seventies, but thankfully there was not much evidence of it at Maine Road. Nevertheless every Saturday night there were reports on the News of running battles between "fans" and railway carriages on the "football specials" were vandalised up and down the country. In this context it is amazing that such protective

70

parents as mum and dad gave me the green light to start to follow City away from home. But this is what they did! My first solo venture took me to Elland Road, Leeds a week after the Wembley defeat to Wolves. The thrill of going to the game was accompanied by a certain amount of adrenalin due no doubt to the element of danger involved. I went by Yelloway coach, which left Middleton at twelve thirty to make the relatively short journey up the M62 to Leeds. As we left the motorway and approached the ground the whole coach seemed to go quiet, or so it seemed to me. The driver pulled up behind the tiny shed of a stand, which was to house the City supporters, and told us that he would return after the game to pick us up. The turnstiles were only just opening as I gingerly emerged from the coach. I had decided prior to the game that I would not stand with the hard core of City support, but that I would stand in the paddock in the Lowfields stand which ran alongside the pitch. I figured that it would be better to stand amongst the older middle-aged supporters who I thought would not be on the look out for trouble, and that I would not make my allegiances known. This was a policy that I would stick to, and which was only difficult when City actually scored a goal.

There did not seem to be too many City fans at Leeds that day. Indeed only one coach left Middleton, perhaps a hangover from the Wembley defeat a week earlier. As the two teams took the field I was certainly in a minority of one in the paddock, and in these days just prior to the segregation of rival fans there did not seem to be more than about a thousand behind the goals in the cowshed. It was brilliant to see City live in their famous red and black stripes for the first time. Leeds paraded their usual "kick everything that moves" brand of football. Billy Bremner, Jack

71

Charlton and Norman Hunter were the main protagonists, but City with Doyley, Buzzer and Frannie did not exactly just roll over and lay down. It was a typically hard fought game which Leeds just edged 1-0.

About five minutes from time I got real butterflies in my stomach. A feeling that I would learn to cope with over the next few years. The Leeds fans sang "it was time for us to run". I was not even anxious about whether City would equalise or not. It was a matter of getting home in one piece! My imagination was running riot. Would there be a waiting party of Leeds hooligans making us run the gauntlet? Would they brick the windows of the coach? Or, worst of all, would the coach even turn up? I left the ground together with a happy middle-aged crowd who were busy arranging their evening out, or arranging to meet in a fortnight at the next home game. They all turned left for their cars, buses or walk into town, and I alone turned right to meet………….Nothing much really. About twenty City fans huddled against the wall awaiting the arrival of the coach. There were the usual grumbles that accompanied a defeat, and the occasional jeer from a Leeds fan or two as they walked past. But certainly no headline misbehaviour. Nevertheless the few minutes waiting seemed interminable to me before our coach eventually pulled up. We all shuffled on board and apart from a defiant chant from the back row, as the coach pulled away the journey home was short, quiet and unremarkable. As we left the coach in Middleton I felt as though I had just become a man! I celebrated with a bag of chips from Tommy's chippy and arrived home as a hero, no doubt to the relief of my parents.

The Cup Final defeat perhaps gave some justification to the belief of Manager Ron Saunders and Chairman Peter Swales that changes were needed if City were to re-establish themselves as a major force in the English game. Their view that City's all-star forward line was past its sell-by date was not shared by the majority of fans. Yet Saunders pulled off a real coup with his signing of Dennis Tueart from Sunderland. This was a very complicated deal with the Blues also taking midfielder Mick Horswill with Tony Towers going up to Sunderland. Tueart proved to be a tremendous signing but Horswill played a mere dozen games, and hardly featured in a winning side. But most of all it was hard to see such a young talent as Mancunian Towers go, as many felt that he was on the verge of an England cap, and a ready made replacement for Alan Oakes who was nearing the end of a great career.

Tueart and Horswill made their debuts in a bad tempered rearranged Derby match on a foul night, which matched the mood of both struggling teams. The game ended goalless, and was notable for the fact that referee Thomas had to take both teams from the field when Mike Doyle and Lou Macari refused to leave it themselves after being sent off!

City were beginning to slip down the table with only one win in the nine games which followed the Wembley final, and attendances at Maine Road fell to 21000 for the visit of Newcastle on the 27th of March. This could be explained by the fact that this was one of four consecutive home games in ten days, but I believe that the majority of fans sensed that all was not well behind the scenes. Nevertheless I attended all four with Macker and Dave Moore, as we built up our new routine of the number 17 bus to town, the Match bus at Aytoun Street, and our new position in the corner of the Kippax at the North Stand end. Francis Lee scored his first League goals for months as Newcastle were beaten 2-1 in a game notable for the

73

substitute appearance of Tony Whelan. It was rare to see a black footballer appearing in English football at this time, and it appalled me to witness the amount of racist vitriol aimed at opponents whereas home players were roundly cheered. There were monkey chants, bananas were thrown and the National Front were regularly in evidence outside First Division grounds. Throughout these difficult times City had a proud reputation of bringing through youngsters such as Tony Whelan, Alex Williams, Clive Wilson, and Dave Bennett all the way from the Youth side to the First Team. But it was only when West Brom later paraded the great Cyrille Regis, Laurie Cunningham and Brendan Batson in their side that fans started to judge black players on their merits. But even they were christened the "Three Degrees"! And by their own manager!

City were by now hovering just above the relegation zone, and Saunders' disciplinarian views were at considerable odds with the experienced members of the team. Relationships were at an all time low, and Swales feared that City would not win another game. With only four games remaining including two against Liverpool and one against fellow strugglers United Saunders was sensationally sacked and Tony Book installed as manager! The Easter visit of Liverpool was witnessed by a crowd of 43000 and Francis Lee scored to rescue a precious point. A week later West Ham were beaten to banish all fears of relegation, and to set the Blues up for the final match of a troubled season in which three different managers had been at the helm. And the opponents? Manchester United at Old Trafford.

The butterflies arrived earlier than usual for this away trip. The thought of going to Old Trafford for a game that could potentially relegate the Reds without dad or any of my close friends filled me with absolute dread from at least the Monday before. "Pay attention, Keogh!" shouted the History master as I began to daydream of terrace battles halfway through a lesson on the Franco-Prussian War. My last thoughts before sleep each evening replayed over and over the travel arrangements to and from the ground.

Saturday came. I couldn't get through my Rice Crispies at breakfast and tried to concentrate on Football Focus with little success. My brothers could not see what the fuss was about. I unusually gave mum a last hug as I left the house feeling like, without being too disrespectful, a pilot walking out to his Spitfire during the Battle Of Britain. At the bus stop I shuffled uneasily as I listened to the gossip and chit chat of mainly women and teenagers going on their regular Saturday afternoon shopping trip.

The bus arrived and in order to avoid United fans chose not to sit upstairs, but to sit near the front down amongst the shoppers. When we reached Piccadilly I got off and walked briskly across the Gardens towards Oxford Road Station from where I would catch a train right to the ground. There were still two hours to kick off but already there were many groups of eight to ten Reds either mooching around or noisily making their way to the match. Head down I followed the tide of young men in their tank tops, bell bottom jeans, platform shoes and red and white scarves tied more often than not around their wrists. At six foot four it is hard to blend in a crowd but I did my best to appear invisible. The train was packed and I was terrified that I would be brought into conversations about what they were going to do to those Blues today. It was a hot day and with clammy hands I could hardly breathe as I emerged from the train.

The concourse around the stadium was busy and I realised that up to now I had not seen a single City fan. My ticket was for the Stretford Paddock as opposed to the world famous Stretford End. I made sure that I entered the correct turnstiles (that would certainly have blown my cover), and after buying the customary programme walked down to the front, turned to the right and made my way up to the half way line where the players came out. I positioned myself a few steps back right behind the dugout. A truly fantastic view! There was about an hour to go and already there were a good number of supporters in the ground. The sound of jeers and catcalls caused me to lift my head up from my programme. Several suited City players including Alan Oakes and Mike Summerbee had emerged from the tunnel just to sample the atmosphere, or was it to wind up the Reds?

About ten to three the ground was absolutely packed and for the first time there were some chants of "City, City" from the Scoreboard End to my right. A number of City scarves were held aloft but this prompted a pitch invasion as a couple of hundred Reds emerged from the Stretford End and amazingly were able to run the length of the pitch before jumping into the Scoreboard End where a number of scuffles broke out. I cannot believe that on such a highly charged occasion that the police could not have prevented this. The few City fans in the Scoreboard End were scattered and chose not to show themselves throughout the afternoon. Indeed when City scored it was clear that they were outnumbered at that end of the ground.

The game itself was mostly fought out in midfield. City were at full strength, but a struggling United no longer contained Charlton, Best or, of course, Law. New manager Tommy Docherty was building a new side around Martin Buchan, Lou Macari, Sammy Mcilroy and that well known German newspaper Gerry Daly. United had to win and hope that others lost to stay in the First Division, and their football had a little bit more edge than that of City but the game was meandering to a goalless draw when on 81 minutes it happened! Colin Bell picked up the ball in midfield just in front of me and moved purposely into the United half of the field. He had Summerbee to his left and Lee to his right. He played the ball out to Frannie who hit the ball low and hard across the penalty area. Some six yards out stood Denis Law with his back to goal. Instinctively he flicked his heel at the ball and it flew past Stepney into the net. The crowd like Denis himself were stunned. United were down! And only six years after lifting the European Cup. The elderly and middle-aged looked around in bewilderment. Children had tears in their eyes. But as for the teenaged and twenty somethings bent on trouble there was only one thing to do. They were on the pitch before you could say Burnley, Oldham and York City. I was frightened for my City heroes but it was clear that there were no moves towards any of them. Indeed Denis Law was mobbed by incredulous well-wishers one of whom put a Red and White scarf around his neck! Denis left the pitch immediately, the police cleared the arena, and the match restarted. Yet minutes later with the ground in ferment and disbelief the players ran for the tunnel as hundreds invaded for a second time. I myself being only yards away from all this watched events with a mixture, if it is possible, of sheer joy and terror.

The referee abandoned the game and the result stood. United were relegated due to events elsewhere. But this was not announced. In the confusion I left the ground and stayed quite invisible on both bus and train until leaving the number 17 at Kingsway and floating home on an absolute cloud. United were in Division Two and as far as I was concerned we had put them there! It was to be City's last win over United at Old Trafford for 34 years.

SIX.

FRANCIS LEE. JUST LOOK AT HIS FACE.

Summers in the early 1970s were spent largely playing cricket. There was no history of the game in our family, with its humble working class Irish Catholic background. It was football, football, and more football! But I did accompany grandad on a Saturday in his role as groundsman at a local cricket club. He admitted to having no real interest in the game but as I loved being in his company I looked forward to my afternoons on the boundary edge, and my attention was gradually drawn to events in the middle. As my love of the game increased I managed to convert three or four of my soccer mad friends and the field began to double up as Lords or Old Trafford in the long summer holidays. I borrowed a book from the library teaching me all the fielding positions, which directly led to me becoming Captain of the school cricket team. (I was the only boy who knew a slip from a silly mid on!). I would bowl leg-breaks to brother Pete who would bat left-handed but bowl with his right. I have few recollections of these titanic struggles save for the fact that our mutual friend Tony had the heaviest bat in Middleton with a bright yellow handle. He was a fine player, a good footballer, but a magnificent cross-country runner.

At school we had a cricket square that was roped off throughout the winter, and lovingly tended by Paddy the groundsman all year round. What is it about Irish groundsmen? The fact that a state school had either a cricket square or a groundsman seems remarkable today. In fact very few schools even play the game! After representing school on a Saturday morning I would rush home for a quick sandwich before filling my duffel bag with cake, biscuits and orange juice and catching the bus up to Towncroft Avenue to watch Middleton in action. Auntie Margaret's house backed onto the ground and her main claim to fame is that her back bedroom window had been broken by a huge six from the great Basil D'Oliveria who played for Middleton before going on to have a wonderful career with Worcestershire and England. My heroes of the early seventies were the much lesser known figures of Leon Taylor, Mike Linton and Tyrell Gauder. Middleton had a fine side as did Lancashire as I graduated to trips down to "the" Old Trafford to watch such greats as Clive Lloyd, Farokh Engineer, Harry Pilling and Frank Hayes carry all before them in the John Player Sunday League and Gillette Cup.

Sunday mornings were now given over to cricket practice at Higher Blackley Cricket Club. I still had to attend Mass, but this was possible on either Saturday or Sunday evening. I always had the impression that dad thought that you did not score as many points by attending at these unorthodox times. A teacher at school managed to railroad about twenty boys from school into the club, which enabled us to form two junior teams. The club was situated in an unfriendly area of North Manchester along the exotically named Crab Lane. The clubhouse was regularly broken into, and the ground sloped away to the right so much so that if you stood at the wicket you could only see the top of the head of a fielder standing on the boundary. Very often you would hit the ball in that direction and set off running, not knowing if a fielder standing at the bottom of the hill would return the ball. Yet to me this arena was Lords and the Oval all rolled into one. Cricket heaven!

Our junior games would usually take place in midweek leaving the weekends free for the seniors. I found myself Captain of the second team, which included six or seven boys who were a year or two older than me. Our wicket keeper was a seventeen-year-old chain-smoker, to the extent that he smoked on the field during the game. As the bowler was running in he had the last long drags on his cigarette before handing it to me at First Slip, still lit, as the ball flew into his gloves. His timing was superb, and it was only on the rarest of occasions that if the batsman edged the ball towards me that I had to let the fag fall to the floor. By allowing our keeper to smoke and acting as his trusted lieutenant gained myself the street credibility necessary to captain a team of older boys. Yet I cannot understand how the Umpires allowed this to happen week after week.

The summer of 1974 was a particular good one for Higher Blackley Juniors. We made it through to the Cup semi final against opponents from a tough side of town on the same evening as Johan Cruyff's Holland side reached the World Cup Final. I was really disappointed that the fixtures clashed but our game was played in an atmosphere unlike any other cricket match that I have played in. We were greeted at the ground by a fearsome group of local tearaways who let us know in no uncertain terms what they would do to us if we won. We could not place any fielders on the boundary as they were targeted for stone throwing practice. Even their Umpire seemed to question every single decision that ours made, and as we began to come close to their total I actually feared for our safety. The night was closing in, and none of our parents seemed to have arrived to pick us up. It was now that my captaincy really came to the fore. I gathered together all our equipment and gave orders to all our players to be ready to go when I gave the signal. We relayed the message to our two lads out in the middle, and scanned the car park entrance for a friendly pair of car headlights. But none came. As we hit the winning run my worst fears were realised. The pitch was invaded from all sides by Neanderthals who proceeded to pick up the stumps and attack our batsmen. Fortunately they were fleet of foot and thanks to the adrenalin charge of our great victory we all fled the scene in our white flannels and cricket boots, chased by a pack of hounds with murder in their eyes through the streets of North Manchester.

The Final was played on the 11th August on a sun-drenched afternoon in a beautiful setting on the edge of rolling hills. The crowd consisted mainly of our parents, pensioners in deckchairs, and little children eating ice creams. Middle-aged spinsters prepared the teas while two young schoolboys worked overtime in the wooden scoreboard to the left of the pavilion. It was all a far cry from what we had experienced in the semi final. Our only scare came when the League announced that all players must wear whites in the Final, and our star bowler revealed that he could not get into his after too many Friday nights of over indulgence in the local hostelry and curry house. Happily with an hour to spare we managed to get him a pair, we bowled well, and with a rare match winning innings from myself we actually won the Cup. Mum and Dad, who were not really cricket fans, were there to see me hit the winning run. And our wicket keeper did not even smoke a single tab during the match!

August 1974 marked the ending of an era over at Maine Road. It is widely thought that Denis Law's last kick for City was the one, which defeated United in April. But in fact the pre-season Texaco Cup tie against Oldham Athletic was the last City game that he featured in. It appeared that Denis had been informed that he would not hold a regular place in the side and that he would be used sparingly. Having just returned from an England-free World Cup with Scotland he decided to retire at the top there and then. Also playing his last game for City that day was Francis Lee who was sensationally sold to Derby County a few days later! I thought that the whole idea of appointing Tony Book was to keep the old team together, and not allow it to be ruthlessly dismantled as had been suggested by the previous manager. I felt that Book was making a huge mistake in allowing Francis to leave. He had had a magnificent career with both City and England, and I feel that he still had lots to offer. I could not believe it! It is easy to be clever with hindsight but Francis certainly played a major part in Derby winning the championship at the end of the season.

As nobody could know of these imminent departures there was a crowd of only 13000 who attended the match against Oldham, including myself and grandad Keogh. The game was not only memorable for the fact that Denis and Francis were playing their last games for City. It was also to be grandad's last visit to Maine Road to watch his beloved Manchester City. He had supported the Blues faithfully since arriving in England in the early twenties. Over fifty years of support! It must have been with a heavy heart that he walked away to catch the bus home for the last time on that damp August afternoon. The fact that City won with goals from Francis Lee and Dennis Tueart remains immaterial.

A week later the League season was up and running. The sun was beating down as I set out down Kingsway towards the bus stop, my brand new Kippax Street junior season ticket book burning a hole in my pocket. With my sky blue silk scarf tied loosely around my wrist, and United in the Second Division I felt a sense of great optimism as I looked forward to the many contests that lay ahead. Macker, unusually for him, was already there at the bus stop feverishly devouring one of his tangerines that he normally saved until half time. Macker was the master of the unusual snack. At one stage he was known to take a handful of Sugar Puffs in his pocket to the pub! We had a choice of three buses and it was the new orange and white SELNEC number 163 from Heywood that came into view moments later. We paid the children's' tariff of two new pence and charged upstairs onto the top deck, avoiding the back rows of hard salmon coloured plastic seating which replaced those habitually vandalised by much rougher boys than us. Most of the top deck was crowded with shoppers, smokers, and tattooed young lovers with their feet on the seats and their heads in the clouds. We took up our seats lost in conversation about the possible team line-ups.

The season began with two home games against West Ham and Tottenham Hotspur. Myself, Macker and Dave Moore were thrilled to hand over our vouchers from our new season ticket books and took up our new vantage point on the half way line amongst a very "macho" group of bus drivers and their undoubted leader Big Ted. If Big Ted said it was Tuesday then it was Tuesday.

Asa Hartford made his debut in a side that included youngsters Colin Barrett, Jeff Clarke, and Phil Henson who had replaced the injured trio of Glyn Pardoe, Tommy Booth and my own favourite Mike Summerbee. There was a growing feeling that City were going to really do the business this season as they tore apart a weak West Ham side with goals from Rodney Marsh (2), Dennis Tueart and Mike Doyle. Asa and Dennis were particularly impressive that day and the young back four was ably managed by the experienced Mike Doyle.

Three days later Spurs arrived at Maine Road for a game which could be claimed to be "after the Lord Mayors Show". This saying must have been invented for City. A close hard fought game was won one-nil by the Blues with the goal coming from new crowd favourite Asa Hartford. The bus journey home had us arguing over just how many trophies City were going to win. It was agreed that Tony Book had already made City a much harder team to beat while still retaining the flair of previous years. That reasoning was soon blown away as City were trounced 4-0 at Arsenal at the weekend.

The first real test at home was the visit of Liverpool on September 14th. Strange things were happening as the sun was again beating down on Maine Road as it had done on the opening day of the season. The winter of discontent, the three-day week and midweek afternoon kick offs seemed light years away. There were no sponsored logos as City wore their club badges proudly on their chests. They had returned to pale blue socks for the first time since Division 2 days. And the football was electric! Inspired by the strength and trickery of Hartford, the strong running of Bell, and the lightning attacks of Tueart, City crushed this great Liverpool side by two goals to nil in one of the best displays of attacking soccer that I have seen.

Centre half Tommy Booth was out with a long-term back injury, and despite the heroics of young Jeff Clarke and Colin Barrett it was clear that City needed to go into the transfer market. The rather unfashionable Geoff

Hammond was bought from Ipswich for £40000 and he slotted in well at right back. He must have been pinching himself to be in the same side as such greats as Colin Bell and Mike Summerbee. Incredibly in a season where City and United were in different divisions for once, they managed to get drawn against each other in the Third Round of the League Cup at Old Trafford. Seventeen-year-old Peter Barnes found himself on the bench and I found myself in a rather good seat in the Main Stand. I managed to get this ticket and a lift in the car to the game from a neighbour who worked in United's Ticket Office. Foolishly I swaggered into the ground expecting an easy victory. Unfortunately so did a few of our players. United were well clear at the top of Division 2, and Tommy Docherty had assembled a good side including McIlroy, Daly, Greenhoff and new signing Stuart Pearson. Chances were few and far between in the first half. Our best chance fell to Summerbee who was put through on goal but his shot was scuffed and Stepney saved easily. Fifteen minutes from time there were loud appeals for a handball in City's penalty area and as it was Old Trafford and in front of the Stretford End the referee had no alternative but to point to the spot. I hoped against hope but Gerry Daly stroked the ball home to give United victory.

Injuries were starting to bite and Mike Summerbee, Rodney Marsh, Asa Hartford and Dennis Tueart were to miss games over the next few weeks, giving opportunities to youngsters such as Peter Barnes and Barney Daniels in attack. Barnes, whose father Ken served the Blues with such distinction in the Fifties, was an exciting talent who despite his slight frame was very tricky on the ball. He could also deliver a good cross. He made his full debut on October 12th away at Burnley in another narrow defeat but a week later he provided the cross for Mike Summerbee's winner against Luton at Maine Road. City's home form was outstanding and in spite of several away defeats they went top of the League after beating Stoke City 1-0 on the 9th of November. The winner that day was scored by Rodney Marsh who by now had really settled into the side and was arguably playing the best football of his City career. Certainly many fans thought so and he was becoming a real hero on the Kippax. As for me, well the jury was still out. I still thought that he had cost us the championship, and I could not forgive his immature Wembley walk off. Although Colin Bell was probably the hero of most fans it was Mike Summerbee who would always be my number one! Nevertheless the outstanding form of Tueart, who would create a real buzz in the crowd whenever he was on the ball, was beginning to create a whole host of new admirers inside Maine Road and throughout the world of football.

Another heavy defeat this time at Birmingham created the strange situation where City were yo-yoing between first and fourth position in the table week after week depending on whether they were home or away! They returned to top spot after defeating Leicester by four goals to one in a game where City included Barney Daniels for the injured Mike Summerbee. Daniels had been plucked from non-league football and simply did not look like a professional footballer. He looked instead like a cross between Alf Tupper, the Tough of the Track, and Barney Rubble. But on that dismal November day at Maine Road in 1974 he played like a man possessed. He scored two goals, the Leicester defenders could not contain him, and the roof came off the Kippax every time he touched the ball. Ted and the bus drivers had found a new hero and the Football Pink that night acclaimed him as the find of the season. Unfortunately these were the only goals that he was to score for the Blues, as six games later he faded back into obscurity from whence he came. But at least he had had that day. He was unstoppable.

By Christmas City had slipped to eighth in the table, and as the Morecambe and Wise Christmas Show came to an end, and the last of the turkey sandwiches lay heavy on my stomach, my thoughts turned to the Boxing Day fixture at Anfield. As much as I was excited at the prospect of watching City play in front of The Kop, I was terrified of travelling to Liverpool on my own. Public transport was notoriously poor on Bank Holidays but I left myself plenty of time to pick up the Finglands coach outside the bed store on Piccadilly Plaza at half past twelve. The sun was bright but there was a real nip in the air as I joined a motley crew of hungover Blues in the shop doorway, which smelt of stale urine and Christmas Eve's kebabs. I didn't know if everybody was as worried as I was or if they were simply suffering from Christmas hangovers but nobody seemed to speak during the short coach journey.

The coach sped along the East Lancs Road and in no time at all we pulled up alongside the huge park that separates Liverpool and Everton football grounds. The place seemed to be deserted. I was one of the first to step out of the coach, and out of the corner of my eye a solitary newspaper seller seemed to beckon me over to him. Yes he did mean me, I double-checked. "Just stand over here with me a minute son" he advised. His soft scouse brogue did indicate a kindly nature so I did as he asked. I stood beside him about twenty yards from the coach when suddenly all hell broke loose. About a hundred Liverpool fans emerged from behind bushes in a scene from the Wild West and they promptly tore into the City lads emerging from the coach. For a split second I would have given anything for dad to have been there but realised immediately that I was on my own. A real rite of passage! An unholy skirmish took place without a policeman in sight yet this had clearly been pre-planned on the part of the scousers. I thanked the anonymous newspaper seller who clearly had more than an inkling of what was about to happen. He tipped me a wink, gave me a smile, wished me well, and pointed me on my way to the ground. My heart was thumping as I reached the Anfield Road turnstiles only to find them closed, as it was not yet half past one! People had warned me at home to beware of young boys outside the turnstiles asking for the time. A Mancunian reply would result a swift retort " There's one here", and then it would be a good chasing or worse. Fortunately as I was rehearsing my best Scouse accent the gates opened and I scurried in and took up a place near the front where I reasoned the more mature Liverpool fans would stand. There was still no segregation in 1974 so fans were mixed together in the "Away" ends. I bought a programme and the ground filled up.

At the far end the sight of a full Kop was awe-inspiring. It was announced over the tannoy that City's centre forward would be Joe Royle of Everton! I was gob smacked, but in those far off days free of the Internet and even teletext, when news did not travel so fast, players were signed without anybody knowing. Amazingly the Blues side contained six international attackers- Bell, Summerbee, Royle, Marsh, Hartford and Tueart! Yet the balance of the side was wrong and Shankly's side ripped us apart and I was grateful for even a four-one defeat. I was even more grateful to get back on the coach safely, giving a sheepish grin to my bruised and battered colleagues. After a few anxious glances at the bridges on the outskirts for stone throwers, in no time at all I was back on the settee at home exhausted from such an adrenalin charged afternoon. I began to nibble away at a couple of mince pies and tried to read a few pages of a Morecambe and Wise biography, but already my thoughts were turning towards Saturday's home game with Derby County.

It was a crisp winter afternoon as the two teams took to the pitch before a crowd of over forty thousand. Everybody was glued to the figure of the returning hero Francis Lee who had served City so well for so many glorious years. Even this most cynical of football crowds secretly wished him well. It is often said that players returning to their scenes of past glories usually put one over on their former clubs, and I am afraid to say that this was certainly one of those occasions. A hard fought game between two well matched sides stood at one goal each when Francis received the ball a few yards to our left just inside the City half attacking the Platt Lane End. He ghosted past two or three half hearted challenges before unleashing a shot of such ferocity from a good twenty-five yards, that it almost burst the net before Joe Corrigan could move. Along with hundreds along the Kippax I could not help myself clapping in spontaneous applause. Francis simply switched into gear, inspired by the surroundings and occasion, and his instinct did the rest. The Match of the Day commentator described it as he saw it. " Interesting…very interesting….just look at his face….just look at his face!" I guess that Francis must have enjoyed it. City did everything that they could possibly do but they could not force an equaliser. Two defeats in three days was soon to become three as they were dumped out of the F.A. Cup by Newcastle by two goals to nil on the 4th of January.

A back heel from Denis silences Old Trafford. April 1974.

SEVEN.

ENGLAND'S NUMBER ONE.

City travelled to Sheffield United on January the 11th for the first League game of the new year. Yelloways were no longer taking coaches to City away games from Middleton, probably due to the mindless hooliganism of the few who were bent on causing trouble. So instead I again caught a Finglands coach from the centre of Manchester. The coach made swift progress over the Woodhead Pass and I found myself outside Bramall Lane before the turnstiles had opened. I decided to stand in the same place where I stood with grandad a few short years ago. It was this day that I reckoned that I was actually the first person on the terraces. As the turnstile opened I was first into the ground and I ran up to the top of the steps to witness a completely empty ground! Opposite, the cricket pavilion had disappeared and the new stand was not quite ready. The programme blamed its lateness on the three-day week and the shortage of steel. In Sheffield!

There was only a smattering of fans in the ground when the suited City players took to the field. I was alongside the tunnel as they returned to the dressing rooms and held out my programme and pen in the hope of an autograph or two. Even though they passed close by several of City's big name players including Doyle, Marsh and Tueart completely blanked me. Only Joe Corrigan, who had been given such a hard time by the fans and could have been forgiven for walking on by, came over and signed my programme. This made a massive impression on me and when times

93

changed for Joe and he became an international I was especially pleased for him. Taking the trouble to make a fan's day on a miserable January afternoon in Sheffield said a lot about the measure of the man. As far as I was concerned he was certainly England's Number One! I still have this autographed programme some thirty-three years later.

Tommy Booth returned to the City side that day after six months out with back trouble and his goal earned City a well earned point. My favourite referee of the Seventies, the rotund smiling figure of Roger Kirkpatrick denied us a winner by disallowing a goal from King Colin in the last minute. Sheffield United must have fielded the oldest side in the First Division that day including Len Badger, the county cricketer Ted Hemsley who had great sideburns, Eddie Colquhoun, Alan Woodward who must have been born with grey hair, and Bill Dearden. Also in their ranks was the brilliant Tony Currie who surely should have won far more England caps than he did? Perhaps it was because he played for an unfashionable side? On his day he was unstoppable.

A fortnight after knocking City out of the Cup Newcastle United returned to Maine Road. They included in their ranks the great goalscorer and Geordie idol "Supermac" Malcolm Macdonald who always seemed to do well against City. I mention him here though because he had a pair of sideburns that seriously rivalled those sported by Ted Hemsley a week earlier! He was also of course bow legged. But he had a fantastic left foot and he sure could score goals.

The Geordie fans had a poor reputation at this time for crowd trouble and theirs was one of only a handful of grounds that I had no intention of visiting despite my growing obsession with following the Blues. Indeed the Cup Tie had been switched to Maine Road on the orders of the F.A. due to riots the previous season at St. James Park, and this game appeared on the Pools coupon as a home game for Newcastle. But one thing that could be said of the Geordie fans was that they were incredibly loyal and a real hardy bunch. On the day of the League match it was bitterly cold and I was well wrapped up with a polo neck sweater, woollen scarf and overcoat all of which could not prevent the wind chilling me to the bone. Yet some sixteen or seventeen years before fans took to wearing their team's shirts with the advent of the Premier League, I witnessed hundreds of Geordies wearing their trademark black and white shirts with red numbers on their backs oblivious to the sleet and Arctic winds swirling around Moss Side. But they could not inspire their side as City, no doubt still smarting from the Cup defeat, put five past Iam Mcfaul with The King of all Geordies Dennis Tueart bagging a hat trick. Even full back Geoff Hammond hit one like an arrow into the net at the North Stand End. Newcastle were absolutely annihilated by the Blues.

The programme that day contained an in depth focus on the great Colin Bell revealing to one and all that his pet likes included "carpet slippers and a weakness for Western films". Slightly more surprising, yet perhaps not so for the mid seventies, was that the following pages contained pin-ups of entrants for the Miss Manchester City Soccer Queen Competition. Prizes for the eventual winner included a visit to the hairdressers, ten days in Gibraltar, and fifty pounds in cash! (In fact the winner went on to marry TV presenter and soon to be FA spokesman David Davies!). Fans were invited to dance and dine at the Bell-Waldron

95

Restaurant, rent a colour television set for £6.40 a month, and become a member of the City Social Club for only 55 pence.

With a dozen games to go City lay in seventh place in the First Division yet they were only three points behind the leaders. But a glance at the League table showed where their problems lay. At home they had won thirteen, drawn two, and only lost one of their games. But away from home it was a very different story, indeed almost the reverse with only one win, five draws and eight defeats. Looking at the side which travelled to Leeds on the First of March, it is apparent that it was somewhat lop-sided containing as it did five out and out attackers in Summerbee, Bell, Marsh, Royle and Tueart. These players of course were seasoned internationals and household names but clearly knew only one way to play. They threw everything at the opposition week after week. At Maine Road this produced a glorious spectacle, but away from home they left too many gaps and put too much responsibility on the defence.

Manager Tony Book talked honestly in the programme about his initial thoughts on making the step up from being a player in the side. First he talked about the difficulties of handling such extraordinary players and characters such as Lee, Bell and Summerbee. He then, most significantly, acknowledged the new tactics coming into games and likened it to a game of chess. He talked with regret of these new rigid patterns, organisation and one hundred per cent effort, as if he was longing for a bygone age of all out attacking. It is clear from this interview that Tony Book had himself identified the problem with City. But I wonder if he did consider sending out a different kind of side for some away games? A side different not only in attitude but in personnel? After all even in the late sixties Dave Connor was brought in for key matches to play a man marking role. If only City had tried to incorporate just a little bit of the systems and organisation referred to by Tony? Would they have been more successful? But then again they would not be City then, would they? I wonder whether at this point Tony Book refused to sacrifice his own principles of all out attack?

March held the key to the title in 1975 with three consecutive away games. Leeds were level on points with City at the start of the game which, with the opening of the new stand behind the goal to replace the old scratching shed, aroused huge interest and attracted some 47000 being the best crowd of the season at Elland Road. Such was the numbers including great away support meant massive queues to get in. It was pay at the turnstiles even for sell out games such as this. Myself, Dave Moore and Macker missed the first fifteen minutes due to the queuing, but could tell from the cheers inside the ground that the score was one-all. The Leeds side contained many that carried all before them a couple of years earlier including Bremner, Hunter, Madeley, Reaney, Lorimer, Sniffer Clarke and the brilliant Eddie Gray. The match was fast and furious and played hard like a cup-tie. Peter Lorimer, who scored the winner on my last visit, scored both Leeds goals. He could certainly hit a ball. A rare goal from young City full back Willie Donachie earned the Blues a share of the spoils.

A narrow defeat at Leicester the following week put extra pressure on the Blues for their visit on the 15th March to Queens Park Rangers. It was to be my first visit to the capital for a League match. I did not sleep for days. I could not persuade any of my classmates to make the long trip. I guess they thought that I was mad, or maybe their parents put the block on a trip to London. After all, the Provisional I.R.A. were waging a bombing campaign in the capital and it was only a few months since pubs were attacked in Birmingham and Woolwich resulting in heavy civilian casualties. Dad told me how embarrassed it made grandad feel as an Irishman, being so proud to have brought his family up in Manchester. It broke his heart to see his compatriots behaving in such a despicable manner. There was considerable ill feeling against the Irish in Britain. This only really hit home when the Catholic Church at the top of our road was covered in six-foot high anti-Irish graffiti.

The alarm bells from the clock beside my bed told me it was five thirty and I made my way unsteadily towards the bus stop, passing only the milkman who was incongruously whistling cheerfully and tinkling his bottles on a still dark mid March morning. Through half open eyes I watched people boarding the bus as it made its way along the deserted Rochdale Road through Blackley, Harpurhey and Collyhurst, then and now some of the most poverty stricken areas of North Manchester. A mixture of postal workers, market traders and the early shift for the biscuit works at nearby Crumpsall paid the driver and acknowledged familiar faces before disappearing upstairs. Hardly a word was spoken, even between friends. Some carried a flask, others knapsacks, most smoked but all had pinched faces peering through the misty windows at nothing in particular, seemingly accepting their fate for the day. As for me, well my stomach was in knots and my heart was pumping fast. I had to get off the bus just after Smithfield Market, hare across Piccadilly, and catch one of the "Fortys" along Wilmslow Road to pick up the coach which was due to leave Finglands Garage at the top of Platt Lane at seven thirty. I made it with twenty minutes to spare. I bought the Sun or the Mirror from a nearby newsagent and immersed myself in such illicit material with their page three girls, which would never have got past our front door at home. It was the Daily Express for us by order of dad!

The passengers on the coach were ninety per cent male, and mainly aged between 18 and 35. I was amazed to find about half a dozen men travelling singly in their forties or fifties. And there was one guy who seemed to be at least eighty and turned out to be profoundly deaf. What were some of these men doing with their lives? Did their families mind the fact that they were spending ten hours of their Saturdays on a coach for the privilege of watching one and a half hours football played by a team who had only won one game away all season? I guess I kind of admired them in a strange kind of way, and wondered momentarily if this was to be my calling in life? Anyway there was little or no conversation until we hit the M6 somewhere between Knutsford and Sandbach service stations. I was unaware in my innocence that the majority of my fellow devotees would have spent the better part of Friday night downing ten pints of mild or bitter followed by the chip shop, and maybe even a scuffle into the bargain. Hangovers were unknown to me.

My sandwiches disappeared, as did signs for innumerable service stations. The coach would briefly come to life when one crammed full of supporters for another team came into view. The occasional insults were exchanged along with the usual Harvey Smith "V" signs. We could do with a victory. Five hours later the coach parked up besides the White City, a few mumbled instructions were delivered by the driver, and our motley crew hit the streets of the capital. As I was beginning to realise we were again very early, being practically the first coach to arrive from

Manchester. The turnstiles were still closed as we ambled carelessly around the ground. I made sure that I did not align myself with any group who were vociferous in their support of the Blues. But most of all I was delighted that the air of menace present at Old Trafford, Anfield and Elland Road was conspicuous by its absence. The Q.P.R. fans strolling around were simply buying food and chatting! It did not seem to be on their agenda to want to fight us.

I managed to find a van selling chips and what passed for a burger. It was not known as fast food in those days but it did the job. I purchased a programme outside the ground and on scanning the front cover began to wonder if it was official. For some unknown reason the cover consisted of an orange and white checker board design with a photo of four middle aged blokes on a coach who appeared to be going to a wedding. As QPR played in navy blue and white hoops and sported a change kit of red and white quarters I was not sure where the orange came in. But on closer inspection of the photo I recognised manager Dave Sexton, Frank McLintock, Dave Clement and Ian Gillard.

In common with many "Away" ends the terrace behind the goal was uncovered, which usually meant that for the same price as what the home fans were paying you often got a good soaking into the bargain. There were not too many Blues in evidence as the kick off neared. I stood amongst a group of cheerful middle aged blokes who were happy to talk about the relative merits of their old hero Rodney Marsh and their new idol Stan Bowles who was beginning to tear apart First Division defences on his days off from the Betting Shop. Indeed along with Dave Thomas, Gerry Francis and Don Rogers he gave City a taste of their own medicine. QPR played their own brand of exciting attacking soccer to beat City by two goals to nil with Rogers scoring both goals. They were a similar side to City because on their day they could give anyone a good hiding with their aforementioned flair players, but they also like City had a fine goalkeeper in Phil Parkes and some real hard men in defence like David Webb, Frank McLintock and Ian Gillard.

I had had a brilliant day, but as I trooped back to the coach I knew in my heart that this result probably meant that the League title would not be going to Maine Road that season. There was a real sense of gloom on the coach as we waited for everyone to board. One by one the coaches began to leave the car park. But we were not moving. One or two fans were growing a little impatient until the driver informed us that the eighty year old had not returned. As unkind comments filled the air I began to worry. "We'll give him five more minutes", offered the driver. Then all of a sudden there he was strolling into the car park without a care in the world. The whole coach erupted with the loudest cheer of the day. He smiled and waved at us all and walked on by. We all fell about laughing as the driver left the vehicle to run after him and bring him back so we could begin the long journey home. The mood of despair had been broken and our love of our club had returned. A chant of "We'll support you evermore" filled the coach. As we got further up the M1 tiredness set in, conversation petered out and we were left with our own private thoughts.

I was by now reaching the end of my years of compulsory schooling with my G.C.E. exams fast approaching. The beatings were becoming a little thinner on the ground. Much of the teaching lacked inspiration and many lessons were spent simply copying from the blackboard with no interaction between teacher and pupils. We studied English and Russian Literature by simply reading the texts around the class, with no attempt at any analysis. The teacher would begin the lesson by asking who read last. We always replied by stating that it was the boy in the register who appeared directly before a lad who had a terrible stammer. Reading aloud for him was absolute purgatory, but the teacher fell for it every time. Was he really that stupid or was he trying to keep in with the wags in the class? This pupil to his eternal credit and to our shame did his level best every time.

"Make sure you bring an orange in with you tomorrow, Keogh, or else." This strange request came from one of the tougher boys in the form and it was one that I made sure I kept. I checked with Macker in the morning and indeed we all had to bring one in and make sure that we eat it at break and bring the peel into lesson two which was English. This particular English teacher was particularly ineffectual and his briefcase was often tampered with and his morning snack removed. " Would you like some chocolate, sir?" "No, thanks. I have got some." "Have you?" replied the pupil half way through sir's Cadbury's Milk Chocolate Bar. This particular lesson we were all in our places and all had our poetry books at the ready. He entered the room as gingerly as ever checking that there were no buckets of water on the top of the door. He could not believe the good order and silence in the room and told us so. He was visibly gaining in confidence as the first two or three boys read the opening stanzas. He probably was thinking that, yes after all, teaching was his true vocation. Then we heard the order… "One, Two, Three….." All of a sudden thirty two boys unleashed the orange peel that they had been sweatily holding on their knees. It flew through the air in a strange slow motion, like orange snow, before covering the hapless teacher from head to toe. He left the room immediately, and the school soon after.

One thing was certain. If you wanted to keep in with the "in crowd" in class then you had to watch "Monty Python's Flying Circus." They knew every word of every joke in every episode. The trouble was that when I asked at home if we could watch it my parents could not get past the naked man playing the organ in the opening sequence. I learned much later that it was Terry Jones, and along with John Cleese, Eric Idle, and Michael Palin he became a huge favourite of mine. It was only by watching constant repeats that I too learnt word for word the likes of the Dead Parrott sketch, the Spanish Inquisition, and the Ministry of Funny Walks (which mum at least admitted to finding remotely funny).

Bus rides home from school were enlivened on evenings when Macker's Grandma boarded it in the centre of Middleton for the short ride home. She was usually quite tipsy having spent the whole of the lunchtime session in a town centre pub. The fact that they closed in the afternoons meant that she was shown the door just at the time when a bus would be pulling up crammed full with Grammar schoolboys from her beloved grandson's school. " Do you know him?" she would enquire of the nearest boy as she tumbled into his lap. "If you see him, give him this," she continued, holding out a ten pence piece. Macker made sure that he caught a later bus, but would tell us of how his grandma was a lunchtime regular and would belt out hymns such as "The Old Rugged Cross" to one and all in the tap rooms of Middleton. She even claimed to have shared a taxi from Middleton with Peter Sutcliffe, the Yorkshire Ripper, whom she added was

103

dressed in drag and when he opened his handbag to pay the fare a hammer fell out. Needless to say grandma claimed to have run like the wind to her cottage on the edge of the woods.

The week after my trip to Queens Park Rangers none other than Carlisle United, who were spending a solitary year in the top flight, put the final nail into City's title aspirations by coming away from Maine Road with two points courtesy of a 2-1 win. Unbelievable! In fact the Blues were to win only four of their last eleven games, thereby finishing in a disappointing eighth place in Division One. Crowd favourite Colin Bell played in all forty two League games and finished top scorer with fifteen goals. Only just behind him came Dennis Tueart who in his first full season in the top division scored fourteen. I was elated that big Joe Corrigan had re-established himself in goal and that Tommy Booth was fit again. There was also the emergence of young Peter Barnes who I had seen make a full debut in the narrow defeat at Burnley back in October. My only sadness was that this probably had an effect on the fact that my personal favourite Mike Summerbee had lost his place in the side and was to be transferred in summer to lowly Burnley for a small fee. But life went on and I truly believed that if we could only tighten up at the back then the title would soon be ours.

The G.C.E. exams came and went and although a few classmates actually left school, the majority of us took it as read that we would return in September as Sixth Formers. The end of the year was to be marked by a school dance or disco as they were now to be called. Unfortunately as we were a boys' school it meant that a joint venture with a girls Catholic Grammar school would have to be arranged. I do not know if they tossed a

risk games. It was a sad state of affairs that you could no longer stand wherever you wanted on the Kippax. I would not be able to wander into the corner by the Platt Lane stand where Margaret and grandad had stood every other weekend throughout the Fifties. This area of the ground was for visiting supporters only! The Manchester derby was the first of half a dozen matches where the gates were firmly bolted some twenty yards or so to the left of the half way line.

With all the pre-match talk centring on what might happen off the field my new partner in crime Phil and I decided to buy two seats in the North Stand for this one. We had barely taken our seats a few rows behind "Big Helen" with the bell, when young United full back Jimmy Nicholl running back towards his own goal gently clipped the ball back to keeper Stepney. Unfortunately for Nicholl and to our sheer delight, Stepney was off his line and the ball sailed over his head and into the net right in front of us. The game absolutely exploded as United hit City with wave upon wave of attacks and they not only equalised through McCreery, but went ahead a minute later with a header from the tiny Macari. Our seats were so low down in the North Stand that we saw all the goals through the netting of the goal and the Platt Lane seemed a long way away. In the very next attack City forced a corner and Joe Royle scored a great goal to make it 2-2 at half time. What a game! The second half passed in a blur and there was no further scoring. The general feeling was that it had been a great match between two good teams and the media was pleased that it had all passed off peacefully on and off the field.

Two days later City travelled to Stamford Bridge for a League Cup Second Replay against Norwich City. There were no penalty shoot-outs in

1975! Not surprisingly only six thousand attended this game at a neutral ground, but those who did witnessed a 6-1 victory for City with Dennis Tueart scoring a hat trick. It was my birthday and I was at a cinema on Deansgate in Manchester watching a film called "Earthquake". The seats actually moved! Or did they?

The following Saturday City achieved a rare feat. Not only did they win an away League match, but it was against Arsenal at Highbury before a feeble crowd of only 24000. The Blues wore black shorts and won by three goals to two with goals from Asa Hartford, Joe Royle, and Rodney Marsh. This was to be City's last victory at the famous old stadium that closed some thirty years later.

It also marked Marsh's last ever goal for the Blues. He had played in all twelve of City's League games and scored four goals, but it was clear that as a player he divided opinions like no other in the stands and on the terraces of Maine Road. At the back of the Kippax terraces where fans often were divided along sectarian divides in their chants of "Celtic" and "Rangers", it was clear that Rodney had created new and possibly irreconcilable divisions. When some fans started up their favourite Rodney chants others would boo or chant the name of Mike Doyle in opposition. Perhaps he represented everything that Rodney did not.   He was a no-thrills hard man born and bred in Manchester with blue blood cursing through his veins. There must have been problems behind the scenes that in a less technological age fans were not privy to. On Monday 13th October the news broke that Tony Book had placed Rodney on the transfer list, (although it was to be some weeks before he was to eventually leave the Blues for America)! That night coincided with a rare First Team friendly at

Stockport County. On a wet night City sent out a strong side, which did not contain Rodney and which significantly included Doyle as Captain. I made my one and only visit to Edgeley Park and found the stadium to be incredibly bleak, chiefly wooden in structure and in need of a coat of paint. It looked better from the train window on the main Manchester to London Euston line. Soaked through in the open end I questioned my sanity, but was rewarded by a great display from the Blues and a five nil victory capped by a hat trick from the great Colin Bell.

Rodney Marsh was an extremely gifted player who scored 56 goals from 142 appearances. Not a bad return. He was an absolute idol for many supporters and lit up many a drab game at Maine Road and elsewhere. My favourite game would have to be the day he beat Derby County on his own on the last day of the season in 1972. But I am left with the feeling that he did not really come off for the Blues. His inclusion disrupted a title bound side, his Wembley walk off upset many, and it had to be said that coming off the back of the most successful period in the club's history City did not win a trophy with Rodney in the team.

Until Joe Royle could return from injury, City played out three draws with both Dave Watson and Tommy Booth filling in up front. To their credit they did more than this in that they each scored a point saving goal at Spurs and Sheffield United respectively. Royle returned against Birmingham and the Blues won their first match without Rodney. Four days later one of the most significant matches in the history of Manchester City took place. Having disposed of Norwich and Notts Forest, the Blues were drawn against United and the tie was to take place on Wednesday November 12th.

113

Tommy Doc's United had made a thrilling return to the top division and as we took up our places alongside the bus drivers on the half way line, it was clear that the Kippax was far more packed than usual. You could not put your hands in your pockets. We were like sardines. We could see the players waiting in the dimly lit tunnel opposite, and I must confess that my heart was in my mouth as they emerged to a full-throated roar by all those present. United's attack was in awesome form but it was their rookie goalkeeper Paddy Roche who was known for the occasional howler who gave us most hope. In fact City attacked from the kick off and Dennis Tueart put us ahead inside 30 seconds. The place went mad. Phil, Dave and I ended up six steps nearer the pitch. Macker meanwhile had obtained a ticket for the Platt Lane Stand, which was full of Reds, so there were no overt celebrations from him. Five minutes later Dennis fed Colin Bell with a through ball and he bore down on goal. Martin Buchan, the stylish United captain, thudded into him and the ball ran loose. Colin went down and the referee blew for a free kick just outside the penalty area. What a chance to go two up! But there was something wrong. Colin was motionless on the floor. Usually just the trainer would run on to tend an injured player. But within seconds several were on the pitch including Tony Book and the club doctor and physio. A stretcher was called for and Bell left the pitch to a great ovation. Nobody realised the seriousness of the injury at the time, and most fans were absorbed with a match that City had complete control over. Substitute Tommy Booth proved just how versatile he was by slotting smoothly into midfield, and by half time City were three goals up with goals from Asa Hartford and Dennis Tueart. On the terraces we were in dreamland and a further goal from Joe Royle completed the rout. To this day this display must count as one of the most complete by the Blues in a Manchester derby. We caught up with Macker who could now express his unconfined joy as we sung our way over to the Parkside pub to catch the match bus back to Manchester. By now most United fans had left early and would have been tucked up in bed. Ha! Ha!

The extent of Colin Bell's injury was not apparent and it was thought that he would be back in the New Year. But the injury that he sustained that November night was so severe that, despite several attempted comebacks by Colin, it would effectively end the career of one of City's greatest players. With the sale of both Lee and Summerbee it also signified the end of City's holy trinity. The three England Internationals had served their club with such great distinction, and along with their team mates brought the club an unparalleled run of success, winning trophy after trophy in the late sixties and early seventies. Colin Bell, such is the man, did not give in easily. He worked and worked to get himself fit and no man could have done more in his attempts to get back to the First Division. Looking at the programme from the derby match, it is a little bit spooky to see a photograph of Colin himself screaming for a stretcher for the injured Pardoe in the Old Trafford derby of 1970.

By the end of the month City were at last beginning to put some consistency together. Even without the transfer listed Marsh and injured Bell they had managed to remain unbeaten in ten League games. On the 29th November I made my first visit to Molineux for the game against Wolverhampton Wanderers. A very funny thing happened on the way to the ground, but it could have turned very nasty. As the coach was travelling through the outskirts of Wolverhampton it got caught in traffic behind a bus. I was sat near the front of the coach and saw a youth open the emergency door on the top deck of the bus and spit on our front window. Now coach drivers are notoriously proud of their transport and may even look after them better than they do their wives, but nobody expected what happened next. Our driver, who years later actually drove the team coach, pulled alongside the bus which was packed with Saturday shoppers, and remonstrated with their driver for him to pull over. Our driver then promptly left our coach, boarded the bus and went upstairs and gave the terrified youth a piece of his mind. The lad was lucky he escaped without a good hiding. The driver returned to the coach to a great ovation and without batting an eyelid drove us to the stadium car park. We were among the first to enter the ground and stood half way up the away terrace behind the goal to the right of the main stand. We were thrilled to learn in school on Monday that when they went round the grounds at half time on ITV's World Of Sport, the camera stayed on us throughout the report. We were really pleased, as there was considerable kudos to be gained from attending an Away match.

Wolves were struggling near the bottom of the League but their side that day contained the experience of Geoff Palmer, Mike Bailey, Frank Munro, John McAlle, Kenny Hibbitt, John Richards and Steve Kindon. They also fielded future City misfit Steve Daley who was to cost us an absolute fortune and never did a thing for us. It was a bitterly cold day at Molineux but the performance served up by the Blues certainly warmed our hearts. Our defence of Clements, Donachie, Doyle and Watson was rock solid, our midfield containing three left footers in Oakes, Hartford and

Power was creative and our wingers Barnes and Tueart were electric. Joe Royle led the line and Big Joe Corrigan kept goal. We won easily by four goals to nil with goals from young Peter Barnes, Dennis Tueart, and two from Asa Hartford. One goal that day really stood out for me. As we fired a corner into the penalty area Mike Doyle came hurtling through towards the near post to flick the ball across goal. But in the process absolutely flattened the referee who could not possibly have seen the ball toe poked into the goal. Yet the goal stood. Wolves looked a sorry outfit and I was delighted that we had gained some revenge for that Wembley defeat. Travelling back up the motorway both Phil and I were convinced as we stared out into the pitch black evening that City were on the verge of something big.

A kind draw in the next round of the League Cup paired City with Mansfield Town at Maine Road. Despite a spirited performance class eventually told and we found ourselves in the semi finals courtesy of a victory by four goals to two.

We were drawn against Middlesbrough with the Away Leg coming smack bang in the middle of my January exams. I had returned to school the previous September as a sixth former. To be precise I was in Lower Six Arts studying French, Russian and History. I still had to wear uniform, the only concession being that a plain black blazer replaced the old one with red trimmings. I made sure that I wore at least one City badge in my lapel. This hardly made me a rebel without a cause, but I can say that at that moment the fixture list of Manchester City was far more important to me than any of my lessons. On the January day that City had to go to

Ayresome Park, I had a History exam that was not scheduled to finish until half past four. Nevertheless I went ahead and bought myself a ticket.

On Friday nights I had started to play five a side football in the school gym with some mates from my class and some older guys who all had jobs in the real world. One particular night I was getting changed into my kit, when the doors flew open and a very confident fellow with flowing locks strolled in and asked me if his mate Chris Finn played here. I glanced across and said that indeed he did and he was just warming up with the others. "My name is Ron" he replied gruffly and started to get changed. I ran in to the gym and stroked one into the bottom corner with my usual nonchalance. "How many players have we got?" someone shouted. I counted up just as this bald guy entered the gym. " Eight, nine, and Ron is still getting changed. That makes ten." I replied. There were a few sniggers and a few of the lads looked at the floor. "That is Ron who has just come in. He always arrives last because he takes his wig off before coming onto the pitch", whispered Dave Moore as the game kicked off.

I was sitting in the exam hall with one eye on the clock and the other on my new Red and Black scarf, which I had fixed onto the wall bars beside me. I had arranged to cadge a lift up to Middlesbrough with some of the lads from Friday night football. They had all booked the afternoon off work and it was my only chance of making the kick off. As soon as the exam finished I got up from my chair before being dismissed, grabbed my scarf, put on my brown corduroy coat, and raced out to the front of the school. It was quite deserted as all the buses had left at least half an hour ago. It was a misty, wet, January evening. A toot of a horn and a grunt from a lowered window meant that my car was waiting. As I clambered

118

into the back seat my friend Chris who had accompanied me to Wembley in 1974 made the introductions. "And I think that you have already met the driver, Ron?" he concluded. Ron turned round, and gave me a knowing grin. At the speed he set off at I thought we would be there in twenty minutes. I think that he was trying to teach me a lesson. You are with the big boys now school kid. I remember that night in the gym. I noticed that the wig was conspicuous by its absence. I wondered if it was in the glove compartment. As we made our way up the Great North Road passing a Little Chef or two the rain began to get much heavier and the mist really came down. I started to wonder if the game would actually take place. We pulled into a side street. It was ten past seven. Ron had done us proud. We took up our seats in the corner of the Main Stand and it was very clear that there were not too many City fans in a sell out crowd of 35000.

Middlesbrough were managed by Jack Charlton at the time and their side were a clear reflection of him. They were hard, dour, and took no prisoners. Not for them the flair of Tueart, Hartford, Barnes and Colin Bell. Their defence contained stalwarts such as John Craggs, Terry Cooper and Stuart Boam. In midfield we were up against Graeme Souness and Bobby Murdoch. Up front they had the experience of John Hickton and David Armstrong who must have played for them for at least thirty years. Matinee idols they were not. Like Maine Road the stadium was surrounded by row upon row of terrace houses. The ground had standing on three sides of the pitch, and the stand we were in was chiefly wooden in structure with little or no legroom between the wooden seats. Hot Bovril and pies seemed to be the order of the day! The ground was packed out. The fans behind the goals were steaming in the rain as the floodlights tried to pierce through the gloom. The atmosphere was electric as the sides took to the field. The great prize at stake was a trip to Wembley! I felt as if time had stood still. This could easily have been the nineteen fifties.

Middlesbrough threw everything at City in the first half. We were lucky to get nil. Joe Corrigan and the recalled Tommy Booth were heroes and chiefly responsible for the fact that the half remained goalless. We held out until sixty-six minutes when Hickton put Boro ahead. The ground erupted and the stand seemed to shake. It seemed like a re-run of "Earthquake." The game ended soon after, and seeing as how City hardly crossed the half way line we had to be pleased with the result. Ron soon hit the road again and in no time at all we were in a pub on the Yorkshire border drinking Youngers Tartan Bitter. I sipped my beer and despite the fact that I was now over six foot tall and accompanied by three twenty year olds, I felt like the schoolboy that I was, and was waiting for the landlord to put his hand on my shoulder and enquire after my date of birth. I hoped that I concealed this from Ron and the lads who by now were in good spirits and looking forward to the return leg the following Wednesday. Wembley was in our sights.

Wednesday 21st January 1976 was one of those nights when everything went right. It was a great night to be a Blue. Middlesbrough were at full strength and must have fancied their chances when they saw the City line up. Dave Watson had not recovered and Kenny Clements deputised for him at centre half with Colin Barrett coming in for a rare start. (He was shortly to leave for Brian Clough's Nottingham Forest where he achieved great success.) Youngsters Barnes and Power kept their places and were joined by twenty-year-old Ged Keegan in midfield. Starman

Dennis Tueart was serving a suspension for a sending off in an F.A. Cup tie against lowly Hartlepool. Many, including myself, feared that this might prove costly. Tueart was in great form and whenever he was on the ball there was a feeling in the crowd that something was going to happen.

Although there were only 44000 in the ground, some eight thousand below capacity, the Kippax was crammed full. The seemingly ever present drizzle filled the air, and you could cut the tension with a knife. I do not know whether Middlesbrough were instructed to sit back and soak up City pressure, but whatever their match plan it was soon in shreds as City took a two goal lead within the first twelve minutes. Peter Barnes danced down the left wing towards the North Stand and clipped the ball back across the six-yard line where the diminutive Ged Keegan popped up unmarked to send what seemed an involuntary header past Jim Platt and into the net. Before the defence had time to recover the ball made its way to the edge of the Boro penalty area where it was met by the mighty left foot of veteran Alan Oakes and the ball screamed into the net. The Kippax went mad. It seemed as if the crowd and the players were one, and that there was nothing that could stop us marching on to Wembley. Peter Barnes and Joe Royle added further goals and as the final whistle went people were hugging and kissing each other. We were at Wembley! A great tidal wave of joy carried one and all through the tunnel at the back of the stand, out through the huge gates, along the passage behind the North Stand, across a crowded forecourt, down the terraced streets and onto the buses into Manchester. We were the famous Man City and we were going to Wembley! As I sat down on the bus I paused to get my programme out of my pocket. And there we were on the front cover! Just above Mike Doyle's left shoulder could be made out the expectant teenage mugshots of Phil, myself and Macker!

NINE.

THE KING OF ALL GEORDIES.

The Wembley countdown had begun and our first objective was to obtain match tickets. As a season ticket holder all I had to do was to tear a voucher from my book and send it with the princely sum of £1-50 to Maine Road. Phil was able to do the same, and we waited in anticipation for our stamped addressed envelopes to fall on our respective doormats. The next thing we needed were souvenirs, so on the first day of the February half term holiday we went down to the souvenir shop at the ground. The area around Maine Road was eerily quiet compared to match day, but there was plenty of activity in the small shop alongside the City Social Club. I decided upon a new silk scarf and both of us bought plastic blue and white bowler hats. I affixed a sticker on mine which bore the legend "Doyle eats Magpies" which seemed to be the slogan adopted by the local media which chiefly consisted of Piccadilly Radio and the Manchester Evening News. We were in such high spirits that we decided to pop in the historic Middleton hostelry "The Old Boar's Head" for a pint to celebrate. An hour later we crossed the road and sat on the steps of Jubilee Park proudly observing the rooftops and chimneys of our home town. We were at peace with ourselves and the world. This was what it must feel like to be grown up. We said our goodbyes with only the twin towers of Wembley in our minds.

Things were not so straightforward for Manager Tony Book. He had one or two real selection problems. Only three weeks before the big day full back Kenny Clements was withdrawn after 70 minutes of a poor display against Aston Villa. There were hints in the press the next day that he may have lost his chance of playing in the Final. The media were pushing the claims of Tommy Booth whose great versatility was clearly an asset to the side. And there was of course young Ged Keegan who had not let anybody down. But the biggest question hung over the fitness or otherwise of the great Colin Bell. The Manchester Evening News revealed that the original injury had " all but cleared up," and that a reserve team game had been specifically arranged to give Bell a run out on the Monday before the Final. Indeed Colin was pictured alongside Dave Watson and Dennis Tueart in his Cup Final suit. With hindsight this seems incredible.

City's League form had spluttered a little since their long unbeaten run came to an end with successive defeats against Leeds and Liverpool over the Christmas period. But a week before Wembley everything came together with a three goal victory over Everton. A great all round team performance was capped with goals from Hartford, Royle and Tueart. The teamsheet significantly had Ged Keegan at right back ignoring the claims of Clements, Barrett and indeed Geoff Hammond who had fallen completely out of favour. Tommy Booth wore the number eight shirt, which indicated that Colin Bell had sadly lost his three month fight for fitness. The side which defeated Everton was announced later in the week to be the Cup Final line up.

The great day dawned cold and grey but I had a real spring in my step as I boarded the coach for Wembley. The pressure for tickets meant only Phil and I were travelling from Middleton. I felt like an old campaigner, because after all it was my third London trip in two years. We had lost the previous two against Wolves and Q.P.R. but this meant nothing. There was real hope in my heart that we would be bringing home the trophy. The coach sped past a blur of service stations exotically named Sandbach, Knutsford, Keele, Hilton Park and Toddington. All places that I had never heard of, famous now to one and all for their bacon sandwiches and cardboard cups of coffee with lolly sticks masquerading as spoons. It was around lunchtime that we hit Wembley Way and turned into the vast coach park. Like many fans and indeed players before me I vowed to make the most of this day and tried to savour every minute. So instead of running straight into the ground I persuaded Phil to enjoy the atmosphere outside. As we wandered around we Blues seemed to be outnumbered by about ten to one. What was it about the Geordies? We decided to make our way around to the East Terrace. Our tickets were for the same end of the ground as last time, but this time Entrance 13 placed us in the top tier of the stand.

One glance at the front cover of the programme told me that we were going to win. The City team group looked confident and assured. The photo was probably taken in pre-season, containing as it did Rodney Marsh and a suntan or two. In complete contrast the Newcastle team look frozen stiff. Their photo looks as if it was taken on a frosty school playing field. A schoolmaster would at least have told them all to tuck their shirts in. Only three of the players are smiling and just Malcolm Macdonald looked confident of victory. But he was like that. "We will beat these lot easily" Tommy Booth seems to be saying to Glyn Pardoe. The programme told us about the "On the Ball" Penalty Prize competition which we hoped would relieve the monotony of several marching bands. The four lucky boys took their penalties against the great Peter Shilton and we cheered on a lad from

125

Stockport. I hope he was a Blue. The other three who came from Harrogate, Luton and Willington were probably all Reds.

In no time at all the teams took to the field and City attacked our end of the ground. After ten minutes or so we took the lead when Joe Royle won a header to nod the ball down for young Peter Barnes to rifle the ball past Mahoney. Phil and I lost our bowler hats in the melee, reminding me of the days when everybody wore caps and threw them in the air when a goal was scored. They probably did not care which cap they got back, but me and Phil were lucky. In fact our bowlers were in our mouth when just before half time Supermac crossed from the right and ex-Red Alan Gowling drove it past Big Joe. There was again that split second of absolute silence before thirty thousand Geordies almost lifted the roof off the stadium. One goal each. Half time. I had only just got back from the toilets, or what passed for them, when Willie Donachie attacked strongly down the left before crossing a high ball to the far post. Tommy Booth leapt early and with his arms on the shoulder of a Newcastle defender headed the ball back across goal. I let out a groan of exasperation as Dennis Tueart shaped to do an overhead kick. But he connected beautifully and the ball was nestling in the back of the Newcastle net. One of the best goals ever scored at Wembley and I thought it was destined for Row Z. I am sorry Dennis. I owe you an apology.

"Dennis Tueart, the king of all Geordies," sang the East Terrace in unison. This really knocked the stuffing out of Newcastle who had obviously gone in at half time with their tails up. Mike Doyle kept Supermac quiet and the final whistle was blown by referee Jack Taylor. Phil and I danced with delight. To see captain Mike Doyle walk up those famous steps and lift the trophy aloft was a boyhood dream come true. My thoughts went immediately to my grandad who had supported the club since 1923. This one is for you, I reckoned with real tears in my eyes. I was not alone as everybody enjoyed their own special moment. The team went on their lap of honour and even Helen Turner who rang her bell at Maine Road was allowed onto the pitch to join in the celebrations. My thoughts went to Kenny Clements who had played right back all season but had to be content with substitute. And of course to the fantastic Colin Bell. The Geordie fans were excellent in defeat and shook hands with many Blues as we all made our way back to the coaches.

The Sunday papers devoured and the highlights of the game on T. V. having finished, I caught the bus down to a very cold Albert Square in Manchester to await our returning heroes on their open top bus victory parade. I must confess that it was a strange affair. Rather like the countdown on New Years Eve. A lot of waiting around in a packed crowd for a few fleeting images of the team with the Cup on the balcony of the Town Hall. My toes were numb with the cold and being dog tired from the previous day I decided that I would not bother with this bit the next time. Next time???

City's return to League action brought a typically mixed bag of results. We picked up four home victories but only two goalless draws out of the remaining seven away fixtures. Sheffield United were easily brushed aside by four goals to nil and Wolves were beaten 3-2 with young Gary Owen making a fine debut in midfield. But it was on the 10th of April that Colin Bell made his largely unheralded comeback against Derby County at Maine Road. It was a quite sensational game with tempers flaring on both sides. The Blues were free scoring at home and raced into a three goal lead inside twenty minutes with goals from Tueart, Royle and Power. But a few yards in front of us in the Kippax there were some tasty tackles flying in, and it was clear that there was no love lost between Mike Doyle and the brilliant yet fiery Leighton James. Both were booked and then Doyle was sent off leaving the Blues with only ten men for most of the match. This Derby side contained many great players from Mcfarland and Todd at the back, Gemmill and Rioch in midfield, and James and Francis Lee up front. They had a real go at City. Bruce Rioch scored two for Derby and the pressure was on. I can honestly say that I had not seen a more bad tempered display than that from James that afternoon. A pity because he had so much talent. How he managed to stay on the pitch I will never know. Dennis Tueart popped up with another goal ten minutes from time to make the game safe but even then Derby scored another. In typical City style we hung on to collect the points.

In such a rip roaring game Bell's contribution was minimal yet understandable considering his long lay off. He was played at right full back and it was clear to all that he did not have the full mobility of his left leg. In fact he had a pronounced limp and shuffled around the pitch. This was a real shock to supporters who did not really know the extent of his injury. Yes, we expected him to be rusty after a long lay off but it was really sad to see our hero struggling through the game. A week later I made my customary trip over the Pennines to Elland Road where Colin scored a superb goal from twenty yards out. But he was a mere shadow of himself. What was strange to me was that the papers, including the Football Pink, made no overt reference to the difficulties that Colin was

128

having just getting around the pitch. So unless you attended the games you were none the wiser. I believe that everybody loved Colin so much that it would have seemed cruel to do so, and that everybody was simply praying for him to fully recover. But it broke my heart to see him playing like this, and no doubt others too.

The season came to an end with a crushing home defeat by a David Fairclough inspired Liverpool. They won by courtesy of three late goals, but to be honest they completely outplayed City. This was very unusual and hard to take but it was no surprise to me when they won the League a couple of weeks later. If this was the standard then we still had some way to go. The final match of the season brought disappointment in a two nil defeat at Old Trafford, but it provided me with one of the funniest things I have ever witnessed in a Football ground. United had lost the F.A. Cup Final against rank outsiders Southampton at the weekend and they bizarrely did a lap of honour around the pitch carrying a cardboard F.A. Cup! I guess our players could not stop laughing either as they meekly folded in the second half. Despite the defeat it had been a great season, what with Wembley and the fact that most home games the Blues scored three or four goals. You could say that my Kippax Junior Season Ticket at five pounds had been pretty good value for money!

I decided that it was time to try to earn some money. Mum and dad financed my away trips, but some of the lads at school had Saturday jobs and were starting to talk about going on holiday. I did not want to miss out so I started looking around for a part-time job. I had one bizarre interview for a job in the café at Boggart Hole Clough. The proprietor was so creepy that when his back was turned I literally made a run for it. I was relieved to find that he did not let the dogs out after me. The café was deep in the park and I was sweating "cobs" when I finally reached safety in the form of Rochdale Road. I managed to find work stacking shelves in a local supermarket. I had to do three nights a week and all day Saturday for the magnificent sum of £8-32 pence. Most of the other lads were full time in the warehouse and soon got to calling me the "Professor" due to the fact that I attended the grammar school. But we all got on well. I was issued with a blue overall and a dreaded "Stanley" knife for cutting open the cardboard boxes. The lads soon showed me the perks for the job, such as dropping a packet of chocolate biscuits and hiding the broken ones behind the tins of peas. Each lad opened a can of coke and hid them amongst the racks of bacon for a crafty drink throughout the evening. This was real life on the edge stuff. Far better than translating passages of French. It was such an adventure that members of my family took to coming into the store on Saturdays just to see me working. The only sour note came one Monday evening when a double delivery arrived at the depot and the foreman locked the doors until we had finished. Instead of arriving home at quarter past eight it was almost eleven when I got in. I had not been able to phone and needless to say mum was "having kittens". But I saved up my hard earned cash and booked a week in Torquay in August with pals Phil and Pete Crowther.

I do not know if it was fate, but we had to meet in the town centre and catch a Yelloway coach at midnight for our long awaited first holiday without parents. The same coach firm and rendezvous as on that distant October day in 1966 when I first went to Maine Road with dad. We decided to go to the "Boars Head" for a couple of beers before the journey.

130

Our parents dropped us off and we asked the landlord if we could put our cases just inside the front door of the pub. Pretty cheeky really as we were all still some months off our eighteenth birthdays which was the legal drinking age. It was a hot August night and we were still unused to beer and I swear that the coach made several unscheduled stops on the long journey down to Devon. We had booked Dinner, Bed and Breakfast in a small hotel just off the promenade, which set us back twenty eight pounds for the week. We were just boys really and the landlady in the hotel became our mum for the week and seemed genuinely concerned for our welfare when we went out. We must have looked so young and awkward in our attempts to look like men. After dinner we would shower, splash ourselves all over in Brut, Aramis, or some other exotic after shave and put on our flared suits and open necked penny round shirts. We hit the pubs every night and even ventured into a disco or two where we stood nightly against the walls listening to the strains of "Young hearts, run free" by Candi Staton, " Silly Love Songs" by Paul McCartney, and "Blinded by the Light" by Manfred Mann's Earthband among others. We would watch in envy as sun tanned beach boys made it look so easy in chatting up the sun kissed disco divas. Pete Crowther made a couple of weak attempts at actually engaging a female in conversation. Phil and I remained rooted to the spot, feeling very much out of our depth. At the end of the second night we all sat down and had a "meeting", where we decided that our failure to even talk to the opposite sex was to remain a secret between the three of us and from that moment on we would simply just get on with our holiday. And this we did. We hit the beach during the day, getting pretty burnt in that hot August of 1976; we had endless games of pool, far too many drinks, and had a pretty fantastic time. We left Middleton as boys, and returned a week later……..as boys.

Homage to The Beatles. Aged 16 in Torquay 1975.

TEN.

THE LIFE OF BRIAN.

It was sad to see Alan Oakes leave for Chester during the summer after seventeen years as a first team regular in which he amassed 561 appearances. He was very unlucky not to play for England. It was a pity that his heyday coincided with that of the great Bobby Moore and Norman "bites your legs" Hunter. Alan was certainly an unsung hero and an integral part of City's greatest ever side.

There were to be three new signings, all experienced players. City signed Jimmy Conway from Fulham who could occupy the right side of midfield; Mick (son of Tommy) Docherty who they thought could fill the problem right back role, and local boy Brian Kidd formerly of United but actually signed from Arsenal. While some Blues were naturally sceptical of signing anybody with Man United associations I was actually delighted because "Kiddo" lived just up the road in Alkrington, Middleton. It was unheard of in 1976 for a First Division footballer to live on an ordinary road in North Manchester. Even back then the majority of City and United players would live in the leafy Cheshire suburbs behind huge fences. But Brian Kidd was a Collyhurst lad and was really down to earth. Yet I must admit that I was rendered speechless on one occasion when I was waiting at the bus stop in my City scarf, bell bottom jeans and Gaberdine raincoat, when his car pulled up and he asked me if I needed a lift to the ground! To be driven to the match by one of City's star players was simply unbelievable. I felt totally inadequate and tongue tied as we discussed the forthcoming game. I mean, he was actually playing in it! He even wished me good luck as I left the car and scurried around to the Kippax turnstiles.

As the City team took the field for the first home match I was astonished to see that they were wearing their new kit, which for the first time included sky blue shorts! Another new feature was a fence in front of the Kippax Street terraces, which although not very high compared to some, which followed at other First Division grounds, nevertheless represented a sad sign of the times. The Blues made a strong start to the season losing only one of the first ten League games. On the 15th of September we entertained the great Juventus in the first Round of the UEFA Cup. It was fantastic to see players like Dino Zoff, Gentile, Causio, Scirea and Boningsena in their famous black and white stripes. The occasion took on a dreamlike quality but the game itself was a tight dour affair like many European evenings. My dad, an ex United fan, had warned me that it would be so, but being a City fan I had not experienced too many of these nights. After half an hour of both teams cancelling each other out, Tueart broke free of his shackles and sent a cross over which Joe Royle flicked on for Kiddo to head past Zoff and give City a narrow victory. Unfortunately it would not be enough, for two weeks later on the day of my eighteenth birthday City went down by two goals in Turin and out of Europe without so much of a whimper. Zoff did not have to get his knees dirty.

My disappointment was short lived as late that night on BBC2 was to be screened an "Arena" special consisting of a Bob Dylan concert from his current American Tour. This represented my first opportunity to see my new hero on stage. Since hearing Bob in that record shop in Torquay twelve months earlier I had been actively seeking out his music. I already owned George Harrison's triple album "The Concert for Bangla Desh" but I had previously only listened to George's songs, which took up the majority of the set. But now I turned to Side 5 and heard George's introduction " And now I'd like to bring on a friend of us all, Mr. Bob Dylan." Bob took to the stage and played five of his Sixties classics. The answer my friend was indeed blowing in the grooves of the vinyl. It was never off the turntable. I lay awake late at night with my transistor radio on my pillow hoping to catch a track from the new Dylan album "Desire" on the John Peel show. I talked about Bob ceaselessly and started to convert brother Pete and friends at school to my new obsession. I no doubt bored the pants off most others. The Arena concert did not let me down. The rain beat down incessantly as it did on Manchester's Kippax while a bearded Dylan, in headgear that mirrored one of the Apostles or a Middle Eastern terrorist depending on your persuasion, reinvented a number of his back pages and several songs off his previous masterpiece "Blood on the tracks". He duetted with his old flame Joan Baez and I was later disappointed to find that these songs had been left off the "live" album that was released some weeks later.

Thursday the 30th September was a big night for me. Along with my usual group of City cronies I made my way into Manchester to celebrate my "eighteenth." For inexperienced lads like us there was not too much choice as far as nightclubs went. It was either the hip and trendy as in "Pips" or "Placemate 7", or the traditional cabaret venues such as " Fagin's" or The "Bier Keller". We would meet in pubs such as The Oxford if we were going along Oxford Road, The Boardroom for Piccadilly, or The

135

Swan with Two Necks for Shudehill. We chose The Swan as we were headed for "Pips" on the corner of Fennel Street near the Cathedral. As we queued up outside we had to invent our dates of birth to make sure that if any of the bouncers asked us our age we were old enough to get in. Obviously I was OK with it being my birthday, but some of the other clubs required you to be twenty one years old to gain admission. It was vital that our maths was spot on. Another problem was that they were reluctant to let in groups of lads. So we would leave the pub in twos and threes and rendezvous inside the club if we were successful. It was like a scene from the "Great Escape" as we celebrated inside at the bar, yet still fearful of a hand on our shoulder meaning that we had been caught.

The club consisted of several small rooms in the basement and we would stumble from one to another in a haze as the night wore on. There was no doubt that our favourite was the Bowie and Roxy room. This was where the best looking girls were, and where the best music was played. The girls, as they danced to "Virginia Plain", "Love is the Drug", and "Jean Genie", seemed as if they came from another planet and were unattainable for the likes of us. Yet the D.J. looked familiar. It was Jon Richmond from the Lower Sixth at school. He was only sixteen yet manning the decks at the trendiest club in town. It was no surprise to me that he later went on to become one of the world's most famous fashion designers. He was just so pale and interesting. So Bowie and Roxy. On the other hand we were just so nineteen fifties and ever so provincial. We should have been more at home in the Soul room where the rougher boys usually congregated. If there ever was any fighting then it usually started to the background of a Marvin Gaye, Jimmy Ruffin or James Brown track. But we fancied ourselves as being far too sophisticated for any rough stuff and anyway we were rubbish fighters. A real bunch of jessies. As the slow smoochie numbers started at around ten to two we grabbed our coats and headed for the exits and made our way up Market Street for a hot dog and the all night bus home.

One or two of our friends had jobs in the real world. They worked in banks or in local government. They had more money than the rest of us and strangely they seemed to prefer the more traditional clubs such as "Fagins" on Oxford Road. This meant that sometimes we had to forget our delusions of the alternative society as manifested on a Thursday night in "Pips", and take a step back into the sixties or even fifties by attending a typical Saturday night's cabaret. Suits and ties were compulsory. As we met up in the Oxford we found to our consternation that one of us had forgotten to bring a tie and did not have a cat in hell's chance of getting in. We could have told him to go home, but it was his birthday that we were celebrating. I volunteered to remove the belt from my trousers and he wore it as a tie. A cheer erupted from the bar area as he made his entrance but it was soon extinguished as the penguin suited bouncers gave us the evil eye. We bought our pints of mild and bitter and sat all eight of us around a table near the dance floor. I looked around. The place was packed out with mostly middle-aged couples eating chicken in a basket. The entertainment consisted of a number of acts such as a heavily made up female singer belting out themes from James Bond films, a comic who did not quite pass the audition for Granada's hit show "The Comedians", and a third rate pop band who had one hit in 1964. In between the disc jockey would spin mainly sixties hits. It was all pretty awful but I thought that this must be how it was supposed to be. A Saturday night out in a Northern town. That particular night at least had a half decent band topping the bill. Their drummer unusually did all the singing and a bit of clowning around. A few months later he had left the band and was a T.V. star in his own right. None other than Russ Abbott.

I was not about to let this new found hectic social life interfere with the serious business of watching Manchester City. By the end of October with City lying in second place in the Division I had already attended four away games but had yet to see them win on their travels. Their brilliant home form was again accounting for most of the points. I saw them hammered by three goals to nil at Villa in the League Cup and three days later made the long trip down to Highbury, to watch what must have been the most boring goalless draw in the history of British football against Arsenal. An excellent draw with Everton was followed by the long trip to Ipswich on the 23rd of October.

By now I was getting used to travelling alone. It seemed that Phil, Macker and Dave, although fanatical about the Blues and season ticket holders one and all, they did not carry that gene of madness that was driving me to follow City all around the country week after week. The trip to Ipswich really took me off the beaten track through the likes of Buxton and the Peak District, Chesterfield and its crooked church spire, Mansfield, Peterborough, and all points east. We even stopped in Newark to sample a Danish pastry in its medieval market square. A far cry from avoiding rabid scousers on the fringes of Anfield Road. The journey took around six hours and it was somewhat of a relief when we eventually pulled up outside Portman Road. The contrast with Maine Road could not have been more

138

striking. We passed a herd of cattle being driven into a nearby field, and narrowly avoided a collision with a combine harvester. This really made me chuckle as City fans used to taunt the country bumpkins from East Anglia with the chant " You are going home by combine harvester."

Ipswich were unbeaten at home and City away, so something had to give. A win would put us top of the League. Kenny Clements had reclaimed his full back slot from Docherty who did not appear again for the Blues, and Gary Owen had replaced Jim Conway who seemed to lack heart. Brian Kidd was still awaiting his first League goal. Ipswich included Paul Cooper, George Burley, Mick Mills, Brian Talbot, Kevin Beattie, John Wark and Trevor Whymark, all of whom would play a huge part in the success of the club over the next few years. City took the field in white shirts with a continental red and black sash, black shorts and black socks. Portman Road was not a lucky ground for City, as they had not won there for years. Despite a brilliant performance from Joe Corrigan, Whymark scored the only goal of the game bringing about our first away defeat in the League. Not bad considering it was the end of October. Dennis Tueart did have the ball in the net near the end but it was disallowed. The bright sunshine of the afternoon had gone down to be replaced by a cold dark early autumn evening. The brief depression of defeat usually lasted about an hour. Mum and dad would take issue with this statement, but as the coach made its long journey north I was already thinking about making a repeat visit to East Anglia as City were to face Norwich the next Saturday. There was nothing but pitch dark out of the coach window and I soon drifted off to sleep.

The weather was much colder and darker as the coach pulled up outside Carrow Road, the home of Norwich City. On the approach to the ground we passed by boats moored on the canal, and watched as weary hikers arrived at their destination at one of the many country pubs dotted amongst the hedgerows. Cows poked their heads through the bushes as if to enquire just what a coach full of city dwellers were doing in these parts. I swear I saw the Two Ronnies leaning over a nearby fence. As if we were in any doubt there were adverts in the match programme for "harvesters for peas and beans" and "animal feed" if we called Dickleburgh 282! Future City manager John Bond in his column bemoaned depressed players who did not like living in Norwich, but went on to express his admiration for the way Tony Book had handled the Rodney Marsh situation. It seemed that everybody in the game knew what had gone on. Tommy Docherty had echoed these sentiments earlier in the season. But the fans were never really told.

I made my way round to the Away section in the corner of the ground. The City fans were singing the theme song from the film "The Vikings" which had recently been shown on T.V. I did not see Kirk Douglas but the locals must have feared a little rape and pillage from these Mancunian invaders. The Norwich crowd themselves were really laid back, almost comatose. Their one song " On the ball, City," was usually sung when they were staring defeat in the face. Their knitted green and yellow scarves and outsized rosettes came from another era. This gentility extended to their team. The likes of Kevin Keelan, Mel Machin, Tony Powell, Phil Boyer and Martin Peters seemed just like a bunch of "nice chaps". They would not have been out of place on a county cricket team.

The referee that day was Bent! Jim Bent from Hemel Hempstead. Kick off was still an hour away as I took up my place on the terraces. There was a huge fence and netting separating the two sets of fans, which made the view of the pitch somewhat difficult unless you went down to the front near the corner flag. This I did where I struck up conversation with a man in his late twenties who I recognised from other away trips.

The game was much tougher than I expected and City seemed more subdued than usual. Dare I say it that they seemed to be far more defensive, certainly from the previous week. Indeed they were booed for the amount of times they played the ball back to goalkeeper Corrigan who was allowed to pick it up before humping it downfield. I would go as far as to say it looked like a new tactic. Is this the price we had to pay for success? The game remained goalless until a few minutes from time when both Joe Royle and Brian Kidd scored at our end of the ground giving the Blues a victory by two goals to nil. I was strangely exhilarated as I danced my way back to the coach park. This time the journey seemed to fly by and as I turned the key in the front door at midnight, mum shouted downstairs as usual " Is that you son?" but then added " I see that they won." Yes it did feel different. A win on our travels! Could this be the year?

Mum revealed that she could not go to sleep until her three sons were all tucked up in bed, so this must have been a difficult time for her as we started to spread our wings. I decided not to tell her about the perils of following City away from home or Piccadilly bus station in the small hours waiting for the all night bus back to Middleton. But she was not daft. She just warned us to be careful. I guess if we were with friends it must have made her feel better. But there was one particular occasion when she expressed her fears about my safety. Strangely enough it concerned a visit to the theatre!

Autumn 1976 marked the grand re-opening of Manchester's magnificent Royal Exchange as a theatre. The opening night was to be marked by a concert by Geordie Alan Price that was to start at midnight after the play had finished. I had seen a programme about Alan Price on television in which he returned to his former school to play a gig for the pupils. I thought the music was fantastic. Apart from the fact that his trademark organ lit up the classic Animals' track "The House of The Rising Sun", he also had a current hit with "The Jarrow Song". I really fancied seeing The Royal Exchange for myself, and loving the idea of a late night concert I bought a ticket. This did not go down well at all at home. Again I could not persuade any of my classmates to come with me. I had already realised that if I really wanted to go to see something then I would have to bite the bullet and go on my own.

I tried my best to ignore the mutterings at mealtimes but could see in mum's eyes that she did not want me to go out so late on my own. I reckoned that if I went to the pub first with friends then this might ease the blow. As I arrived in the Red Lion at about eight o'clock, the mist was starting to gather around the streetlights and it was bitter cold. It was in this pub on the Rochdale Road that some weeks earlier Macker had gone to the bar for the first time and was heard to order "Two pints of beer, please." Everybody around him burst out laughing and when the sympathetic landlord asked him what kind he wanted he made things worse by replying, "Whatever you have got." We usually drank bitter or light mild. In those days there was even a choice of light or dark mild. After four or five pints I made my way out of the pub alone and would have given anything to have made my way home. Instead I made my way through the gloom to the bus stop on the other side of the road. Standing by the park entrance as the fog came down I swear I heard wolves howling and all I could see was mum telling me " I told you so."

After what seemed like an eternity the bus arrived, I boarded and trying to make myself invisible I sat near the door staring out of the window. I scurried across Shudehill turning right down Market Street and after momentarily losing my bearings found myself standing outside the theatre on St. Ann's Square. I was too early. I stood in a doorway examining my new pair of brogues until the hurried footsteps and muffled chatter of theatregoers told me that the play was over. I looked at my watch. It was quarter to midnight. I walked up the flight of stairs in through the huge doors and gave up my ticket. I looked up. I had never seen anything like this before. To my right, high up in the roof you could see the exchange boards from the last day's trading years before! In front of me bathed in blue was what looked like an Apollo spacecraft. This was the theatre itself which was built inside the huge edifice that was the Royal Exchange. It was truly a breathtaking sight. People entered the auditorium from all directions and it was no time before Alan Price struck up the first chords. The concert over, I practically ran onto the first all-night bus and full of adrenalin and on auto pilot, I sprinted along Kingsway, unlocked the door and fell into bed. "Good night, son," whispered mum.

City were on a roll. The team began to pick itself. Paul Power and Gary Owen were both local lads, both left footed, both inexperienced, yet offered different things to the team. Power was very quick and used his pace to great effect down the left wing. He had a great left foot but used his right to stand on. Owen was very tricky; two footed, and preferred to play inside. It was great to see them both embedded in what was in effect becoming a team of Internationals. Corrigan, Doyle, Watson, Royle and Tueart were in the England squad. Donachie and Hartford were capped by Scotland. The team was completed by Brian Kidd, who once he had got the first goal out of the way, began to hit the net regularly. And of course there was Kenny Clements who two years ago was a groundsman at the club! The fantastic future international Peter Barnes could not get in the side.

By Christmas an unchanged team had put together a run of eight games unbeaten. But this was the acid test. Leeds and Liverpool in two days. I was joined by Phil on my now regular excursion over the Pennines on a bitterly cold December afternoon. City were second in the League but Leeds were struggling around the half way mark. Manager Jimmy Armfield blamed their predicament on the amount of injuries that they had suffered. Hardly an original excuse. Leeds still contained a few of their great Seventies side including Paul Reaney, Paul Madeley, Peter Lorimer, Alan Clarke and Eddie Gray. These tremendous players were joined in the side by Trevor Cherry, Gordon McQueen, Joe Jordan and Frank Gray so this constituted a formidable team. But they could not replace Billy Bremner and Johnny Giles easily.

The stadium was absolutely packed with a capacity crowd of 48708 creating a magnificent atmosphere. City brought a huge following to the game and the terraces were so packed that Phil and I could not get onto the top step. Now, at six foot four I could see the pitch, but I am afraid to say that for the first twenty minutes or so, all that Phil saw was when the orange ball was in the air. I had to commentate to him what was happening. City were outmuscling the mighty Leeds and seemed just too quick for them. It was no surprise when Mike Doyle hit a long ball forward (which Phil saw) for Brian Kidd to run onto and hammer home. Twenty minutes later it was Two-nil with Kidd again the scorer. The crowd surged forward and Phil and I saw our chance and jumped onto the terrace from where we watched what was indeed an easy victory. Such was our dominance was that we could have scored four or five. This was what champions were made of!

Two nights later Liverpool were the visitors to Maine Road, and if I am honest the game should never have taken place. The winter had begun to really bite. In the afternoon after the sun went down it began to freeze. Washing left on clothes lines became as stiff as a board, intricate patterns of ice frosted the window panes and the pavements were really treacherous. As we got off the match bus people were slipping and sliding in their efforts to reach the turnstiles. What the open corners of the Kippax were like I could not imagine. Yet it was clear that the crowd was massive, topping fifty thousand for the first time that season. Perhaps this was the reason why the game did take place. City were again unchanged and throughout this fine run only used substitute Barnes in three games. Liverpool were at the top of their game. This was the Liverpool of Kevin Keegan, Emlyn Hughes, Tommy Smith, Ray Clemence, Steve Heighway and Terry Mcdermott, Jimmy Case, Phil Neal and David Fairclough. The pitch was covered in frost and the teams played with an orange ball as they did in 1968 in the "ballet on ice" against Tottenham. Within minutes it was clear that this would be no ballet. The players could not stand up and our match of the season was turning out to be an absolute lottery. The ball bobbled unkindly and if slightly over hit the receiver of the ball had no chance of keeping possession. The atmosphere was nevertheless intense. We all knew that this was our chance to not only put one over on our great rivals but also to strike out at the top of the League. Joe Royle put us ahead and there were very few shots on target from either team. Such was the cold I could not feel my toes even though I was wearing two pairs of football socks. I was just starting to think about leaving a bit early, which was something that I had never done, when Liverpool attacked down the left, the cross came over, and somehow Dave Watson nodded the ball back towards Big Joe, who watched as it bobbled over the line and into the net at the Platt Lane End. The crowd was stunned. The whistle went before City could mount an attack and it felt like a defeat as we made our way home through the mist and the falling snow.

ELEVEN.

MY DEAR WATSON.

Such was the ferocity of the weather that City did not play another League game until January the 22nd with fixtures all over the country falling victim to the snow. They did manage to squeeze in two F.A. Cup ties against West Bromwich Albion. The first match at Maine Road ended in a one all draw with the replay taking place three days later on Tuesday 11th of January. The coach journey down was pretty hairy to say the least. The motorway was deserted which led to skid pan conditions and the side roads were blocked with snow. How does the man who drives the snow plough get to work in the morning? The Manchester Evening News referred to the " Arctic like wastes of The Hawthorns" and I would not have been surprised to see a team of huskies leading out the two teams. Our following that night was tremendous and filled the whole of the terrace behind the goal. The Blues fans amused themselves before kick off by indulging in a massive snowball fight. Oxo was consumed in vast quantities and Fishermen's Friends were very popular.

I glanced through the programme but my hands were just so cold. A review of the sporting year hailed the likes of John Curry, David Wilkie, James Hunt, Barry Sheene and Joe Bugner. It also condemned the rising tide of hooliganism and referred to the bankruptcy facing Newport County and Chelsea. It mentioned the new idea of keeping Saturdays free in order to help international managers and looked forward to transfers going through the ceiling. As for West Brom? Well their manager Johnny Giles had put together a very experienced side, which included three Mancunians Len Cantello, Tony Brown, and David Cross, the formidable centre back pairing of John Wile and Alistair Robertson, and Scottish international winger Willie Johnston.

There was a slight covering of snow on the pitch as City attacked the stand where the Blues were all gathered. After twenty minutes Kenny Clements cantered down the line and crossed into the box. Goalkeeper John Osborne dived on the ball but as his elbow hit the bone hard ground he released it right at the feet of Joe Royle. He gleefully hammered it home. City then sat back and despite the home fans booing Mike Doyle for the endless stream of back passes to Corrigan, we held out for a narrow victory. The motorway was actually closed on the way home and it was almost midnight when I arrived back in Manchester. I was in the middle of my mock 'A' Levels that week but as far as I was concerned I had my priorities right. I am not sure that everybody agreed with me!

The bad weather left one or two Saturdays free of football so I decided to take the bus into Manchester. It was indeed a very grey, litter strewn city. At the turn of the year it seemed that the days did not really get light at all before returning to night around four o'clock in the afternoon. I used to wander around the Tib Street area, home of numerous pet shops, market stalls and seedy "health" clubs. Making my way gingerly through the sodden cardboard boxes and rotten fruit, I would pass by the newsagents full of the "dirty mack brigade" thumbing through the magazines on the top shelves and the army regalia emporiums selling everything from Nazi Luger pistols to red jackets from the Crimean War. In amongst the hamsters, gerbils, and rabbits, I was seeking out the second hand vinyl store selling mint copies of Bob Dylan and The Beatles bootleg albums. I was able to purchase such gems as Dylan's "Great White Wonder" album and four sides from the Beatles' lengthy "Let It Be" sessions. They were even sold in brown paper bags, which led to a little embarrassment on the bus home. Another area that I used to frequent was Oxford Road down past the BBC towards the University, where you could get second hand 'A' Level texts and cassette tapes of any concert that you could care to mention. I shrieked with delight at getting my hands on the infamous Bob Dylan 1966 "Judas" tape from the Free Trade Hall at Georges' Record Shop down by the Johnny Roadhouse Music store opposite All Saints Park. On the way back into town I would buy a Donner Kebab from the takeaway alongside the Odeon cinema. I felt very bohemian for an hour or two with my head in the clouds, but as I boarded the bus back home to Middleton reality would sink in and my spirits would sag just a little.

City were back in League action on the 22nd of January with a home fixture against Leicester City. In his programme notes Manager Tony Book bemoaned the fact that the Blues had lost some fixtures to the weather. He claimed quite rightly that it was better to have points in the bag than to have games in hand. He went on to recognise the great away victory down at The Hawthorns and acknowledged that it was chiefly due to the discipline that the team had now injected into their away form. At the half way point in the season City had only lost one away game out of ten and only conceded seven goals. This was most certainly due to the great form of keeper Joe Corrigan, Mike Doyle and Dave Watson. But also it was clear that no chances were being taken by the defence. When they were put under any kind of pressure they were kicking the ball into the stand or playing it back to Big Joe. In my opinion the midfield offered greater protection to the defence and had tempered the notion for all-out attack that had characterised the Blues' play in previous seasons. I believed that the Blues were all set for a real title push and I was intent on going to every fixture that I could be it home or away.

Brian Kidd was hitting a rich vein of form and had scored seven goals in ten games. His displays had earned him the plaudits of Daily Mirror Footballer of the Month, and City fans' Player of the Month for December. He is seen in the programme receiving his award from a smiling Peter Swales. Chairman Swales revealed that the idea of creating the Junior Blues came from the early fifties by the Saturday morning cinema clubs in which youngsters queued around the block to see the likes of Abbott and Costello, Tarzan, Batman and Robin at the local flea pit. The Junior Blues had just enrolled its 5000th member and has gone from strength to strength since then.

Leicester, lining up in all red, had Steve Kember, Keith Weller, Jon Sammels and Frank Worthington in their side but all the flair came from City. The Blues were already one goal up when Dennis Tueart had to leave the field after only 17 minutes. He was replaced by young Peter Barnes who had been patiently waiting for his chance. He turned in a great display of wizardry on the wing running past defenders as if they were not there. Strong running and pin point crosses from Paul Power allied to great finishing from Brian Kidd gave City an easy win by five goals to nil! Kiddo scored four with the other coming from skipper Mike Doyle. Kiddo left the field with the match ball under his arm to the roars of delight from his growing army of admirers on the Kippax. The win left City only three points behind leaders Liverpool but with three games in hand. Brian Kidd now had eleven League goals to his name putting him one goal ahead of Dennis Tueart as City's top scorer. The League was full of top British strikers including Keegan, Toshack, Mariner, MacDonald, Gray, Worthington, Pearson, and Latchford. Otherwise surely Kiddo would have made the England side alongside club colleagues Joe Corrigan, Mike Doyle, Dave Watson, Dennis Tueart and Joe Royle.

There were two consecutive away victories at Newcastle in the Cup and at Stoke in the League where I was amongst a following of over ten thousand Blues. The press referred for the first time to a blue army that marched out of Manchester that day. Tony Book claimed that it was the best travelling support that he could remember since the day that City clinched the title at Newcastle in 1968. The following week City narrowly defeated Arsenal in a bruising encounter at Maine Road, in which the Football Pink claimed that the referee had lost control of the players. This prompted an astonishing attack on City from television pundit Jimmy Hill on "Match Of The Day". He practically called City a dirty team, denounced their negative tactics and actually highlighted popular striker Brian Kidd as the main perpetrator. Jimmy Hill had such a high profile on TV that his words carried much weight and he should have measured them much more carefully. I do not know whether this outburst had a psychological effect on the City players, but it was a very tame performance from the Blues the following week at Ashton Gate against Bristol City where we went down by the solitary goal to a toe poke from

151

Chris Garland. This was a game that everybody expected City to win, and marked the end of a tremendous seventeen game unbeaten run.

I have never seen anybody who could head a ball better than City's Dave Watson. Many a time he would head it from the half way line into the opposing penalty area. But the best header of the lot has to be that which provided the winning goal against leaders Ipswich Town on the 2nd of April. City had stuttered for a few weeks after the Bristol away defeat and significantly Brian Kidd had struggled to find the net. Nevertheless they went into the Ipswich game only three points off the top with a game in hand. City took the field without the injured Doyle and Tueart. Ipswich wore their change colours of yellow shirts and blue shorts. A great first half performance saw City take the lead through Kidd but Ipswich equalised through Whymark after 55 minutes and were clearly on top. Like everybody around us in the Kippax, Macker, Phil, Dave and I were resigned to the fact that we would have to settle for a draw. Then four minutes from the end we won a corner at the North Stand end. Peter Barnes floated the ball towards the back post and Watson leapt above everybody, and with his neck muscles at full stretch sent the ball back in the direction from which it came into the back of the Ipswich net. Everybody went absolutely wild. Watson himself raised his fist above his head and charged back towards the half way line like a man possessed. There were only nine games to go!

Two more goals from Brian Kidd gave City a Good Friday win over Leeds at Maine Road and the next day held the mouth watering prospect of a visit to Anfield for what many considered to be a title decider. I made my way through Piccadilly bus station to catch the coach from outside the large bed store. I was stood with a motley crew of about thirty leaning against the windows reading the match reports from the previous day when suddenly all hell broke loose. A gang of United fans appeared from nowhere and started hitting and kicking us Blues in the middle of a busy crowd of Saturday shoppers. I immediately turned on my heels and ran into the bed store. There were one or two newly wed couples and a startled shop assistant staring at me as I proceeded to test out one of their special offer double divan beds. Two or three United fans entered the store looked around and left. I cannot believe that I actually passed for a prospective purchaser. I grinned sheepishly at the shop assistant and got onto the coach, the skirmish over and no real damage done. This type of hooligan activity was commonplace in the seventies but thankfully got no closer than that with me. I am afraid the afternoon just got worse.

The coach arrived at Anfield at around two o'clock and there were huge queues all around the ground. There were no tickets to buy for the terraces so it was first come first served. I joined a queue for the Anfield Road End in the first instance, but after half an hour and still twenty yards away from the front the turnstiles abruptly closed leaving hundreds of us stranded. The scene was chaotic as people panicked before running around to the famous Kop end. Unfortunately the queues here were even bigger, and as I heard the roar to announce the entry of the teams I was still nowhere near the front. Eventually at about five past three the House Full notices went up and I was locked out!

There were hundreds in the same predicament as me but as I looked around I did not recognise any other City fans. The coach would not be leaving for three hours or so. I did not know what to do. As the crowd thinned out I felt conspicuous as having no real place to go. Even if the pubs had been open it would have been completely out of the question to go into one so near to the Anfield stadium. I decided to walk in no particular direction. I found myself in a cemetery by the park as a huge roar announced a Liverpool goal. I imagined scouse tearaways lurking behind every gravestone. I eventually found my way back to the coach only to find it locked up and without a driver. So off I drifted again around and around the streets of back-to back houses for what seemed like an eternity. Eventually the streets became alive as people left the stadium and I gratefully made my way onto the coach. I was absolutely drained and amazed to find that the majority of those returning had actually got into the ground. How could they have done so when we all arrived together? And the result? Unfortunately we were beaten two-one with a late winner from ex-Blue Steve Heighway. The attendance was 55283. Surely they could have squeezed a few more in?

My early teenage obsession with all things Beatles was coming to a natural end. This was aided by the explosion of Punk, which hit Britain a few months earlier. Tony Wilson at Granada had started showcasing local talent on his new shows "So it goes" and "What's On". Manchester was becoming the place to be. I am honest enough to admit that I did not attend the infamous Sex Pistols concert at The Lesser Free Trade Hall. Any body who has been anybody in Manchester music since that June evening claimed that they were there! But it was the Electric Circus in darkest Collyhurst that was the ultimate punk venue where you could catch gigs by Manchester bands such as The Buzzcocks, Jon the Postman, Warsaw, or the Salford bard John Cooper Clarke. Macker and I indeed caught the mood of the times by attending an early Stranglers gig there, and being good North Manchester lads seemed unaware of the dangers in doing so. We spent the whole evening cowering against a very damp wall in almost total darkness. You could say that we were down in a sewer avoiding a skewer! This was only weeks before bands like The Stranglers moved into concert halls such as the Apollo, and eventually like punk itself The Circus left town.

By early 1977 I had become gripped by the raw excitement of Punk and it was then that divisions between our group of friends started to bite. Some were much more comfortable in the "Fagins" of this world and clubs such as the recently opened opulent "Romanoffs" on Oxford Road, where bouncers would not even let you take your jacket off! But underneath "Fagins" was a basement club named "Rafters" where brother Pete and I ventured to see punk poet John Cooper Clarke. We absolutely loved it! It was not just because he physically was a dead ringer for Bob Dylan in his "Blonde on Blonde" pomp. In fact John was even thinner with legs like pipe cleaners. Neither was it just because we adored the machine gun delivery of his classic poems such as "Beezley Street" and "Evidently Chicken Town". Nor was it just because his Northern themes were spewed forth in an authentic Salford accent. It was a combination of all three. He was absolutely magnificent! "Rafters" was dark, smelly and steaming on a good night. Like most others we paid little attention to support acts as we consumed vast quantities of Harp Lager and went through packets of Benson and Hedges from the cigarette machine at 48p for twenty! Our laziness, intoxication, and ignorance may have caused us to miss the likes of Warsaw who were shortly to be renamed Joy Division. Nevertheless we would try to see Johnny Clarke as often as we could, memorizing as many of his lyrics as possible. As the summer progressed, Bob Geldof's Boomtown Rats and The Jam would play gigs down the road in Middleton Civic Hall. But by the time I bought "Peaches" by The Stranglers and "Do anything you wanna do" by The Rods a few weeks later, afficionados would tell you that punk was over. And I was still wearing flared trousers!

With five games to go City had managed to hang on to Liverpool's shirt tails and were level on fifty points each. Liverpool had a slightly better goal difference and a game in hand. On the 30th of April The Blues travelled to lowly Derby without the suspended Asa Hartford and the injured Dennis Tueart. Old friend Ron who had got rid of the wig and was now a taxi driver offered to drive us down to the Midlands for this crucial match. My heart was in my mouth as he took some of the hairpin bends outside Macclesfield like Graham Hill. He made excellent time and we pulled up outside the Baseball Ground at half past one. "That will be £19-50, lads", he declared pointing to the clock that he had left on since we left Manchester. My mouth went dry as I made a swift calculation. This was an absolute fortune and I did not have enough cash to pay. I looked across at my young City pal Nibby and saw that tears were welling up in his eyes. "Only joking, lads" laughed Ron.

We entered the ground as soon as the turnstiles opened and made our way towards the half way line. The visitors' section was alongside the pitch in those days. I use the term "pitch" very loosely. On that April afternoon it resembled a beach. And I am sorry to say that City proceeded to play like donkeys. Archie Gemmill had a tremendous first half and we were lucky to leave the field goalless. A Dave Watson header did hit the bar, but we hardly put two passes together and were hassled out of our stride by a Derby side who were up for a scrap. Twenty minutes from time Derby scored through Gemmill and City lost the plot completely. A second soon followed from Daniel and then the tackles started flying in, followed by fists on the terraces. The afternoon was turning into a nightmare. Clements, Watson and Kidd were booked before Derby scored a third after 78 minutes. Brian Kidd was sent off for "persistent misconduct" before Owen conceded a penalty. You could not even make out the penalty spot in the heavily sanded area. Nobody in Blue really cared but Big Joe Corrigan started to count out twelve paces. Whether he was doing it sarcastically only he knew but the referee decided to take his name. Some City fans invaded the pitch recalling ugly memories of Old Trafford 1974. The penalty was despatched, order was restored and the final whistle blew. We had lost by four goals to nil. I was just so happy to get back into Ron's taxi and in no time at all we were sat in The Cat and Fiddle on the hills above Buxton, bemoaning the fact that we had thrown the title away. The press had a field day. The Express declared that it was the day that City were stripped of their skill, their ambitions and most of their dignity. I could not argue with this.

But in football as in life, there is always another day. A week later on May the 7th Tottenham Hotspur were the visitors to Maine Road. Time had not been kind to them. The days of Jimmy Greaves, Terry Venables and Dave Mackay were long gone. In fact, a defeat would relegate them to Division Two. The great Pat Jennings was still in goal but the rest of the side, wearing an unfamiliar yellow strip, was unrecognisable from that which I saw on that October day eleven years previously. The team was captained by Steve Perryman, and it contained the experience of Ralph Coates and the youthful talent of Glenn Hoddle amongst others. The atmosphere on the Kippax was really upbeat despite the fact that City were still two points behind Liverpool, who had a ten goal advantage over the Blues which was as good as an extra point. In his programme notes, Tony Book heroically refused to concede the title but with only three games to play the fans knew that the writing was on the wall.

Roared on by a crowd of nearly 38000, a Tommy Booth header gave City a half time lead. It was in the second half that the Blues took the game by the scruff of the neck and pulverised Spurs with a fantastic display of free flowing soccer. Dennis Tueart hammered in a second before Peter Barnes scored one of the finest goals that I have ever seen at Maine Road. He ran through the middle of the Spurs defence, side stepped a last desperate tackle, and shaped as if to shoot. The great Pat Jennings hit the deck and Barnes cheekily lobbed it over him and into an empty net. Asa Hartford and Brian Kidd added further goals to give City a handsome five goal victory. Spurs were down. The City players left the field to a standing ovation. The results from the other games were announced over the loudspeakers. Liverpool had won again. It did not seem to matter. The fans boarded their buses secure in the knowledge that they had been privileged to witness an absolutely fantastic season of attacking football at Maine Road. City had won fifteen, drawn five and only lost one of their home games. They scored thirty eight goals and only conceded thirteen. Brian Kidd top scored with twenty one League goals followed closely by Tueart with eighteen. Despite City drawing and winning their last two games Liverpool made their extra game count and pipped us to the title by just one point.

My days as a schoolboy were coming to an end. I mean, after all I was approaching my nineteenth birthday! The study of texts by French writers such as John Paul Sartre and Albert Camus hinted at both another way of thinking and indeed another way of living. There was a whole new world out there waiting for me. A world glimpsed through a steamed up window of a coach somewhere between Milton Keynes and Newport Pagnall, or in the Manchester cellars of Pips and Rafters. Bob Dylan through the rain at Forth Worth, Texas, or a midnight concert at the Royal Exchange. The "Cherry Orchard" by Chekhov warned me that my comfortable existence would soon be over, and that decisions regarding an uncertain future would have to be made. The order was rapidly fading. Friends like Macker had already decided that he would be leaving for University, and Dave Moore had got himself a job in London. The academic life held little appeal for me, and all that I was concerned about was getting a job which would furnish my nights out, fund a fortnights holiday with the boys in Majorca, and pay for my beloved City season ticket!

On the 16th of August 1977 Elvis Presley died, and I started work in an office in Manchester city centre. The King was dead, but City had signed Mick Channon. The Southampton goal machine and England inside forward. The final piece in the jigsaw. As I made my way to work on that sunny August morning I allowed my mind to wander. To a rain soaked winter afternoon under the Maine Road floodlights. Joe Corrigan diving to his left to knock the ball round the post. A slide tackle from Mike Doyle taking both ball and opponent into the advertising hoardings. A strong run by Neil Young through the inside left channel, followed by a shot that the keeper could not hold. A follow up and tap in by Colin The King after a forty yard dash. Mike Summerbee feinting to go inside before leaving Pejic of Stoke on his backside, before crossing into the box at the Platt Lane End. A nod down by the mighty Wyn Davies and powerful finish from Francis Lee. The Kippax roar…….

I smiled inwardly and recalled a childhood of nothing but blue skies.